BUILDING
YOUR LIFE *on the* BASIC TRUTHS
of CHRISTIANITY

BUILDING

YOUR LIFE *on the* BASIC TRUTHS
of CHRISTIANITY

Larry Kreider

DESTINY IMAGE® PUBLISHERS, INC.
P.O. Box 310, Shippensburg, PA 17257-0310

"Speaking to the Purposes of God for this Generation and for the Generations to Come."

This book and all other Destiny Image, Revival Press, Mercy Place, Fresh Bread, Destiny Image Fiction, and Treasure House books are available at Christian bookstores and distributors worldwide.

For a U.S. bookstore nearest you, call **1-800-722-6774.**

For more information on foreign distributors, call **717-532-3040.**

Or reach us on the Internet: **www.destinyimage.com**

ISBN 10: 0-7684-2749-5

ISBN 13: 978-0-7684-2749-3

For Worldwide Distribution, Printed in the U.S.A.

1 2 3 4 5 6 7 8 9 10 11 / 13 12 11 10 09

DEDICATION

I dedicate this book to my wife LaVerne, to my family, and to the DCFI family worldwide, with whom we have had the privilege of serving the Lord for nearly 30 years. This book is also dedicated to every person who reads this book seeking to lay a strong spiritual foundation in his or her life. And most importantly of all, this book is dedicated to the One who has promised us that He will build His life in us...our Lord Jesus Christ, to whom I am eternally grateful.

For no other foundation can anyone lay than that which is laid, which is Jesus Christ (1 Corinthians 3:11 NKJV).

ACKNOWLEDGMENTS

A very special thanks to my editor and writing assistant, Karen Ruiz, who does a superb job. Also, thanks to the thousands of believers in the DCFI family worldwide who have walked with us as we learned these foundational biblical truths during nearly three decades of serving together. We have been on a journey as we continue to learn to live out these basic truths from the Word of God. Thanks to the numerous spiritual leaders in the Body of Christ at large, from many different denominations, who have offered countless spiritual insights that have helped to shape this book. And a very grateful "thank you" to the DCFI team of leaders, who I have been honored to serve with for more than 25 years and who have labored tirelessly to give me the time to write this book. It is a joy to serve our Lord together with you!

ENDORSEMENTS

Larry Kreider's passion for the Church that Jesus is building is multi-dimensioned. Clearly, as this book indicates, besides being an igniter of evangelism and an initiator of church planting, Pastor Kreider is a leader who instills life-transforming truth in new believers, establishing true disciples for the ongoing growth of God's Kingdom, while resourcing the healthy development of the growing Christian's life and witness.

—Dr. Jack W. Hayford
President, International Foursquare Churches
Chancellor, The King's College and Seminary Founding
Pastor, The Church on the Way

Too often in our churches we neglect the basics. That's why we seem to have such a large number of born-again believers who are dysfunctional. I am elated that Larry Kreider is forcefully bringing us back to the basics in *Discovering the Basic Truths of Christianity* and its sequel, *Building Your Life on the Basic Truths of Christianity*. These two books will cause you to understand what you really believe and how it works out in real life. Larry has provided a wonderful new treasure for the Body of Christ!

—C. Peter Wagner, Chancellor
Wagner Leadership Institute

TABLE OF CONTENTS

INTRODUCTION

Tiger Woods is a professional American golfer whose achievements rank him among the most successful golfers of all time. He is known as a powerful and creative competitor who knows the basics of golfing and performs very accurately and consistently.

As a golfer, and like most athletes, Tiger has developed accuracy and power in his golf swing through building a strong golfing foundation by practicing the basics. At the driving range, he practices his stance, grip, and swing. He practices putting. He practices getting out of sand traps. With countless repetitions, he practices each fundamental element of the game.

No matter how talented or experienced you are, if you want to excel at anything, you have to practice the fundamentals—the essentials. It's true for playing the piano, it's true for playing baseball or golf, and it's true for the Christian life.

In this second of a two-book series, *Building Your Life on the Basics of Christianity,* you will learn how to practice the fundamentals of Christianity by deepening your relationship with God, learning how to relate to others in the Church, serving others, handling money, and reaching out to those around you as you continue to build on the foundation of Jesus Christ and His Word.

The truths from the Word of God are presented with modern-day stories that help you easily understand the basics of Christianity, lay a strong spiritual groundwork, find God's purpose for your life, and experience practical Christian living each day.

Use this book and the first book in this series to lay a solid foundation in your life; if you are already a mature Christian, these two books are great tools to assist you in mentoring others. May His Word become life to you today.

God bless you!

PART I

Learning to Fellowship With God

Chapter 1

KNOWING GOD THROUGH HIS WORD

GETTING TO KNOW HIM

Let's imagine that you are jogging down a street in Washington D.C. and the President of the United States jogs by. You hail him with a greeting, "Hello, Mr. President." Does the president know you? Do you know him? Probably not. You may know all about the president, but it's one thing to know a lot of facts about him; it's a different thing to actually know him personally.

In the same way, many people know all about God, but they don't really know Him in a personal way. God is infinite, the Creator of the universe, the original Being, the sovereign Ruler of all that is. No one created Him (see Acts 17:23-25); He has always been around and will continue eternally unchanged (see Heb. 13:8). How can we get to know this infinite God when we are but finite humans? How can our minds even begin to comprehend Him?

We can get to know God through Jesus Christ. God has made Himself known through Jesus. He is made real to us through a relationship with His Son, whom He sent to earth to do His will. Jesus came to personally encounter us and die for our sins so that we can live forever: *"Now this is eternal life: that they may know you, the only true God, and Jesus Christ, whom you have sent"* (John 17:3).

According to the Bible, eternal life involves getting to know, commune with, and fellowship with our God who is made known through His Son Jesus Christ, whom He sent. God wants to know us personally! In this book, we're going to learn how to fellowship with God through meditating on God's Word and praying and worshiping Him. We will discover how to develop an intimate relationship with God through Jesus Christ.

Beforehand, however, it is important to understand who God is. We believe in and worship one God. When God spoke to Moses in the ancient days, He revealed Himself as One. Centuries later, when Jesus was asked to choose the greatest commandment, Jesus quoted those same words of long ago: *"...Hear, O Israel, the Lord our God, the Lord is one"* (Mark 12:29).

The Bible clearly teaches that there is only one God. Yet we know from Scripture that God is Father, God is Jesus, and God is Spirit. That does not mean that God is three. There is only one God whom we love and worship. So how can He be one and yet three?

WHEN THREE EQUALS ONE

According to the Bible, God is one God who is three persons. The term *Trinity* is used to describe this concept. When Jesus said that we should go into all nations, making disciples, the three persons of the Trinity are linked together: *"...in the name of the Father and of the Son and of the Holy Spirit"* (Matt. 28:19).

The Bible also tells us, in the book of Genesis, that God said, *"Let Us make man in Our image"* (Gen. 1:26). When the world was created, God the Father, God the Son, and God the Holy Spirit worked together to create the earth and all that is on it.

God the Father, God the Son, and God the Holy Spirit always were in existence.

The Father, Son, and Holy Spirit are coequal, coeternal members. Although this concept is not easy for us to understand, our God is one essence existing in three distinct persons who share a divine nature—God our Father who is in Heaven, God the Son whom He sent to earth, and God the Holy Spirit who dwells in every believer who has been born again through faith in Jesus Christ.

The three are not three gods or three parts or expressions of God, but are three persons so completely united that they form the one true and eternal God.[1] To fathom this, our minds and hearts must be stretched to hold a greater God than we can even imagine! God is so great—our finite minds cannot easily understand. It sometimes helps to look at the things that He has created. In nature, we find things that take different forms and have different effects on our senses, yet are still one.

For example, water takes on three different forms. Water is converted into an invisible vapor or gas (steam) by being heated. Ice is the crystalline form of water made solid by cold temperatures. No matter what its form (water, steam, or ice), it is still water.

Another example from nature is the sun. According to scientists, no one has actually seen the sun because it is so powerful. When we look at the sun, we do not see the star itself, but we can clearly see the rays of sun that shine on the earth. From the sun itself, through its rays, we have light and heat, and something mysterious makes plants grow (through the process of photosynthesis). We can conclude that the sun is the sun—one entity. Yet, the sun is light; the sun is heat; the sun is growth-life. All of this is true without contradiction. It is still the sun.

Although these illustrations from creation may help us to understand the idea of God being One—Father, Jesus, Spirit—they are not enough. We cannot decide who God is and what He is like based on what our eyes see, our ears hear, or our hands touch. We must put our faith in God Himself. We must choose what to believe about Him based on His Word.

We must spend our lives seeking Him and getting to know Him better. We must read the Bible and do what it says. How can we understand Him without knowing and loving Him? How can we see Him without believing and obeying Him? No one person can fully explain God to another. We must each seek Him and know Him: *"And without faith it is impossible to please God, because anyone who comes to Him must believe that He exists and that He rewards those who earnestly seek Him"* (Heb. 11:6).

JESUS IS GOD

When we earnestly seek God, we find Him through Jesus Christ. Before getting into the remainder of the chapter, let's look briefly at the claims of Jesus. As Christians, we must believe that He is who He said He is because it persuades us of His deity.

Very few people will say that a man called Jesus of Nazareth never existed. There are many ancient writings, both religious and secular, that confirm His place in history. There are many, however, who will say that He was just a good man or a prophet. Many believe that He was just a man, flesh and blood, like the rest of us. The religious leaders of Jesus' generation thought the same, and they wanted to stone Him. The things that Jesus said made them furious (see John 10:24-38) because Jesus boldly claimed that He was God.

They accused Him of blasphemy because only God has the right to say that He is God.

How can we know that Jesus is who He claimed to be? Jesus' answers to the stone-throwers pointed to four reasons that we can be certain Jesus is who He said He is:

Scripture: Jesus continually pointed to and affirmed the Scripture. He knew the Scriptures and obeyed them. He fulfilled all of the prophecies about the Messiah.

Sonship: According to prophecies, Jesus was born of a virgin in Bethlehem. Jesus called God "Father" and stressed His unique relationship as His only begotten Son.

Actions: Jesus told His accusers not to believe Him unless He did what His Father does. Jesus' whole life was characterized by a constant awareness of the Father's will. He said and did what the Father said and did. Though many tried to accuse Him, they never were able to because He had done no wrong.

Miracles: If none of that will persuade us to believe, the miracles should. He restored sight to the eyes of a man born blind. He made the deaf hear and speak. He made the lame walk, cured lepers, and made many other sick people well. Demons obeyed Him without hesitation, knowing who He was. He had authority over nature, calming a storm with a word. He changed water to wine and multiplied one boy's lunch to feed thousands. He walked on water. He made accurate predictions about what people would do and what events would take place. Greatest of all, Christ rose from the dead. Death could not rule over Him! Jesus' resurrection is the real proof and demonstration of His deity.

It is interesting to see that, with all of Jesus' claims and with all of His power, He never denied that God is One. He simply said that

He and the Father are One. Jesus was not merely a man or prophet. Jesus is who He claimed to be. He is God's Son. He is One with the Father. Because of who He is, Jesus is able to reconcile the world to the Father.

GOD'S WORD IS LIFE

God wants us to get to know Him. The Scriptures say in Revelation 3:20, *"Here I am! I stand at the door and knock. If anyone hears My voice and opens the door, I will come in and eat with him, and he with Me."* This is an invitation! When we receive Jesus, we are invited to sit down to a friendly meal together. This is a picture of the intimacy that God wants to have with us.

How can we build a relationship with Him? First of all, we build a relationship with the Lord by meditating on the Word of God. John 6:63 teaches us, *"The Spirit gives life; the flesh counts for nothing. The words I have spoken to you are spirit and they are life."* Many Christians today find themselves dried up spiritually because they have not taken God's Word as spirit and life. The Bible is not just a set of good principles and historical facts; it is life to us! As we meditate on His Word, we build a relationship with Him. He speaks to us through His Word.

A friend of mine stepped onto an elevator a few years ago, and to his surprise, there stood Billy Graham the renowned evangelist. He only had a split second to ask Mr. Graham one quick question, "Mr. Graham, if you were a young man like me, what word of advice would you have?"

The evangelist looked at him with the sincerity that has marked his life and said, "Read the Bible and get to know the Word of God."

The evangelist had learned, after walking with the Lord for many years, that the best way to know God is to know His Word.

In reality, Jesus and His Word are one: *"In the beginning was the Word, and the Word was with God, and the Word was God"* (John 1:1). To know Jesus is to know His Word. To love Jesus is to love His Word. You cannot separate the Word of God and Jesus Christ. Revelation 19:13b says, *"...His name is the Word of God."*

A few years ago, I read the results of a survey that produced some startling findings. It said that one-quarter of Protestant church leaders in America are not born again Christians and that only half of all church leaders (53 percent) believe that there are moral truths that are absolute.[2] That's one of the reasons why spiritual power has gone from many churches today! If we don't believe that the Bible is the Word of God—that it is actually Jesus speaking to us as His people—we are bankrupt of spiritual power. God will not be able to move supernaturally in our lives. Unbelief will hinder God's supernatural work. Even Jesus could not do many miracles in His hometown because of the unbelief of some of His own family members (see John 7:1-5).

GOD'S WORD RENEWS OUR MINDS

Romans 12:2 says, *"Do not conform any longer to the pattern of this world, but be transformed by the renewing of your mind...."*

What does it mean not to be conformed to the pattern of this world? The *world* mentioned here refers to our present age or world system. This *world* is subject to the devil—the god of this world (see 2 Cor. 4:4) and is consequently filled with sin and suffering.

In this age, satan uses the world's ideas, morality, philosophies, mass media, etc. to oppose God's people and His Word. The world's system is one of selfishness that is under satan's rule. In contrast, God's Kingdom is a Kingdom of love.

One translation of this verse in the Bible says that we should not be "put into the world's mold." Have you ever taken a box of gelatin, mixed it with hot water, and poured it into a mold? After it has time to chill, the gelatin is shaped like the mold. The Bible says that, if we do not separate ourselves from this world's system, we will end up molded like the world.

Renewing our minds is like taking a car with an old engine to a mechanic. After the mechanic puts in new parts and greases and adjusts them correctly, the engine runs like new. If we do not renew our minds by the Word of God by getting "greased and adjusted," we will begin to think and act like the world's system around us. The Word of God actually cleanses our minds from the thoughts and mindsets of the world system around us. It is like taking a spiritual bath on a regular basis. Living in this world causes us to get spiritually dirty. The Word of God cleanses us and renews our minds. Ephesians 5:25-26 tells us, *"...Christ loved the church and gave Himself up for her to make her holy, cleansing her by the washing with water through the word."*

In the Book of Acts, we read that Paul the apostle was impressed when he met a group of people called the Bereans (see Acts 17:10-11). Whenever Paul preached, the Bereans checked it out to see if Paul's teaching coincided with the Scriptures. Whenever you hear the Word of God preached, regardless of who is preaching, realize that it must line up with what God says in His Word. Men and women are fallible, but God's Word can always be trusted. It is always the final authority. We need to study God's Word so that we know the truth (see 2 Tim. 2:15).

GOD'S WORD GIVES US POWER TO LIVE

Some years ago, a friend went to visit one of his neighbors who had been sick for a long time. The neighbor was in a subconscious state and couldn't respond to anyone who came into his room. My friend took his Bible along and began to read the Word of God. An amazing thing happened. For the first time in weeks, the man began to stir. The Word is full of living power: "*...whatever God says to us is full of living power*" (Heb. 4:12 TLB).

Jesus realized that the key to His life was in knowing the Word of God and communing with His Father in Heaven. God has given us the Bible so that we can know the Word of God, apply it to our lives, and defeat the devil. Taking time each day to commune with God and to read His Word protects us from the lies of the enemy. When Jesus was tempted in the wilderness, He said to the devil, in Matthew 4:4, "*...It is written: 'Man does not live on bread alone, but on every word that comes from the mouth of God.'*"

If I receive an e-mail from a person, it is a direct communication from that person. When we read the Word of God, God speaks to us clearly. Jesus and His Word are one (see John 1:1).

A common problem that many Christians experience is finding time to read and meditate on the Word of God each day. The devil and the demons of hell will do everything they can to keep a Christian from studying the Scriptures and communing with the Lord through His Word. God wants us to set aside a specific time to pray and read His Word each day. Take that time seriously and plan for it. It will not just happen.

Reading a Scripture with your bowl of cereal in the morning and then praying for two minutes as you drive to work or school does not really add up to a time of communing with Jesus! However, it is important to start somewhere. Start by reading a few verses each day and expect the Lord to speak to you. Take time to be with your friend, Jesus. As you grow in the Lord, you will want to spend more time with Him.

I have found that, by reading one or two chapters from the New Testament and two or three chapters from the Old Testament each day, I can read through the entire Bible each year. But that is not where I started as a young Christian. I started with what I could handle—several minutes each day.

Those who do not spend time in the Word of God each day become weak. What happens if you do not eat food for a few days? You become physically weak. If we do not meditate on the Word each day, we become spiritually weak.

When we are born again and receive Jesus Christ through faith, our spirit has been reborn by the Spirit of God. Our soul, mind, will, and emotions are being renewed each day by the Word of God as we meditate on His Word.

MEDITATE ON GOD'S WORD

We need Jesus and His Word in our lives each day. Without Him, we can do absolutely nothing, but with Him, we can do all things (see Phil. 4:13). Whenever I do not have the Word of God flowing through my life by daily prayerful study of the Word of God, I find myself growing weak spiritually. I cannot do the things that God has called me to do. Jesus promises in John 15:4-5:

> *Remain in Me, and I will remain in you. No branch can bear fruit by itself; it must remain in the vine. Neither can you bear fruit unless you remain in Me. I am the vine; you are the branches. If a man remains in Me and I in him, he will bear much fruit; apart from Me you can do nothing.*

As we allow the life of God to come into us, communing with Him daily in His Word, our lives will bear spiritual fruit. And that is exactly what the Lord has called us to do—bear fruit.

The Living Bible tells us, *"the backslider gets bored with himself, but the godly man's life is exciting"* (Prov. 14:14). Our lives will be filled with excitement as we get to know God and as we experience His Word helping us to overcome obstacles in our lives. People around us should say, "What do you have? I want it." As we meditate on the Word of God, He builds faith in our lives to do what He has told us to do. We should meditate on His Word day and night:

> *But his delight is in the law of the Lord, and on his law he meditates day and night. He is like a tree planted by streams of water, which yields its fruit in season and whose leaf does not wither. Whatever he does prospers* (Psalm 1:2-3).

The word *meditate* literally means "to reflect on or ponder over."[3] Memorizing the Word is a part of the meditating process. When you and I eat physical food, that food becomes bone, blood, and tissue in our bodies. When we meditate on the Word of God, it spiritually becomes a part of our lives. We begin to act and react the way that Jesus does because of the power that is in His Word. Those who live in the Word of God will produce spiritual fruit.[4] The Bible says in Galatians 5:22-23, *"But the fruit of the Spirit is love, joy, peace, patience, kindness, goodness, faithfulness, gentleness and self-control....*"

All of the fruit of the Holy Spirit will become a very active part of our lives when we meditate on the Word of God each day and commune with Him. Are you meditating on God's Word each day? If not, today is your day to begin.

ENDNOTES

1. *NIV Full Life Study Bible* (Grand Rapids, MI: Zondervan, 1992), 1479.

2. Barna Research Online, www.barna.org, "Leadership" statistics and analysis in this archive come from national surveys conducted by Barna Research, 1997.

3. *Merriam-Webster Online Dictionary,* 11th ed., s.v. "Meditate," www.merriam-webster.com/dictionary/meditate (accessed 29 Sept 2008).

4. For more about the fruit of the Spirit, read Larry Kreider and Sam Smucker, *Exercise the Fruit of the Spirit and Get Fit for Life* (Lititz, PA: House to House Publications, 2008).

KNOWING GOD THROUGH HIS WORD
REFLECTION QUESTIONS

1. According to Hebrews 11:6, how can we really get to know God?

2. Write down the four reasons confirming that Jesus is who He said He is.

3. How do you know when your mind needs to be renewed?

4. How do you feed your spirit so that it may grow?

Chapter 2

KNOWING GOD THROUGH PRAYER AND WORSHIP

OUR COMMUNICATION LINE

Besides meditating on God's Word, another way that we can fellowship with the Lord each day is through prayer. The Lord wants to communicate with us! Ephesians 6:18 says, *"And pray in the Spirit on all occasions with all kinds of prayers and requests. With this in mind, be alert and always keep on praying for all the saints."*

Prayer is our communication line with our God. During war, if a battalion loses contact with headquarters, the soldiers are in serious trouble, becoming much more vulnerable to the enemy. It often works the same way in our Christian lives. We are in a spiritual war. The devil is constantly trying to break down our communication line with God.

Prayer is only as complicated as we make it. God has not asked us to pray fancy prayers. Prayer is simply communication with Him. It is talking with God, sharing our hearts, and listening. God wants us to talk to Him in the same way that we talk to our closest friend. I often write down my prayers, and then I can give praise to God when I see these prayers answered. When we know that God is answering prayer, it builds our faith.

Prayer can take various forms. We can pray in the language we speak (English, Spanish, Swahili, French, etc.) or speak in tongues (our prayer language between us and God, used to build up our spiritual life). Paul is referring to both when he describes how he prays in First Corinthians 14:15: "...*I will pray with my spirit, but I will also pray with my mind....*"

Paul prayed with his spirit, and he prayed with his mind. In other words, a believer can pray with his spirit (in tongues) as the Holy Spirit gives the utterance (see 1 Cor. 12:7,11; Acts 2:4) or pray with his mind (in a known language), also under the impulse of the Holy Spirit.

When our spirits are praying in our heavenly language (in tongues), we are bypassing the devil by using a direct prayer line that God has given to us (see 1 Cor. 14:2). It is equally important to pray prayers directed by God in our own language. Both are needed!

LORD, TEACH US TO PRAY

Jesus lived a lifestyle of prayer. He was constantly in communication and fellowship with His Father in Heaven.

But Jesus often withdrew to lonely places and prayed (Luke 5:16).

...Jesus went out to a mountainside to pray, and spent the night praying to God (Luke 6:12).

The disciples witnessed Jesus' prayer life and wanted it for themselves: "*One day Jesus was praying in a certain place. When He finished, one of His disciples said to Him, 'Lord, teach us to pray...'*" (Luke 11:1).

To my knowledge, the only thing that the disciples actually asked Jesus to teach them was "to pray." They saw how Jesus prayed in secret. Whenever Jesus was involved with people, they saw miracles and wonderful events take place. They knew that there was a direct correlation between His communion with His Father and the supernatural occurrences that they were witnessing. Jesus set the example of listening to the voice of the Holy Spirit to direct Him in every situation. His heavenly Father gave Him the ability to always know just where to go and who to talk and minister to.

A MODEL PRAYER

Jesus gave His disciples a model prayer, which we call *The Lord's Prayer*. The purpose of this prayer was to teach us how to pray. Jesus said in Matthew 6:9-13:

> *In this manner, therefore, pray: Our Father in heaven, hallowed be Your name. Your kingdom come. Your will be done on earth as it is in heaven. Give us this day our daily bread. And forgive us our debts, as we forgive our debtors. And do not lead us into temptation, but deliver us from the evil one. For Yours is the kingdom and the power and the glory forever. Amen* (NKJV).

This prayer has helped me pray throughout nearly 40 years of walking with Jesus. But during the past six years, I have received revelation on the Lord's Prayer that has revolutionized my daily prayer life. The Lord gave me a visual picture of a house with a courtyard in the center and twelve rooms around it, corresponding to the 12 parts of the Lord's Prayer. My book entitled *Building Your Personal House of Prayer* develops that unique plan to go through the twelve rooms corresponding to each part of the Lord's Prayer.[1] Let's look at key components of this prayer briefly.

We enter the "family room," where our heavenly Father is waiting for us. *"Our Father in heaven..."* is never too busy to see us.

In the "adoration room" we acknowledge that God is holy, *"...hallowed be Your name,"* and we tell Him how much we love Him.

We enter the "declaration room" and pray, *"Your kingdom come."* Our deep and abiding knowledge that God reigns in our hearts and transforms us into His likeness causes us to declare that God's Kingdom will come and that His will will be accomplished in our families, our communities, our church, our schools, our places of business, our small groups, and literally everywhere we go.

"Your will be done on earth as it is in heaven." In the "surrender room," we trust the details of our lives to God. We pray for God's will to be done in our lives here on earth as we surrender all to Him.

In the "provision room," we pray, *"Give us this day our daily bread."* We are asking for the things that we need. God wants us to ask. He tells us that *"we have not because we ask not"* (see James 4:2).

"Forgive us our debts...." In the "forgiveness room" we allow God to search our hearts. We consider our sin, God's forgiveness, and how to access that forgiveness.

In the "freedom room," *"as we forgive our debtors,"* we realize that the Lord wants us to have freedom in all areas of our lives. To obtain this freedom, we must forgive anyone who has sinned against us. If we do not forgive, God cannot forgive us (see Matt. 6:14-15).

In the "protection room" we pray, *"do not lead us into temptation...."* We are saying, "God, I ask you to lead me and carry me, so that I do not fall into temptation. I depend totally on You to keep me from sin."

"...but deliver us from the evil one." In the "warfare room," we are reminded of the truth that the Lord has called us to stand against the powers of darkness in Jesus' name. That is why the Word of God tells us that we should resist the devil and that he will flee from us (see James 4:7).

Jesus closes this model prayer by declaring, *"For Yours is the kingdom...."* In the "Kingdom room" we realize that we are citizens of the Kingdom of God and that we are His sons and daughters. We live out this reign each day by living as active members of the community of Jesus—loving our enemies, forgiving those who wrong us, healing the sick, feeding the hungry, and confronting sin.

"...and the power and the glory forever. Amen." The Lord's Prayer starts and closes by giving honor and glory to our God through Jesus Christ. In this "power room," we enter into the fullness of what God has planned for our lives—to be plugged into the power source of the Holy Spirit operating in our lives and in the lives of those we are praying for.

LET YOUR REQUESTS BE KNOWN

The Bible teaches us to pray without ceasing (see 1 Thess. 5:17). We need to be in a constant attitude of prayer, whether we are at work, home, school, or spending time with friends. We can pray on the way to the office or while cutting the grass. Jesus gives us this advice in Luke 11:9-10:

...Ask and it will be given to you; seek and you will find; knock and the door will be opened to you. For everyone who asks receives; he who seeks finds; and to him who knocks, the door will be opened.

If you lost a check with a whole week's wages, how long would you search for it? You probably would search until you found it. We need the same tenacity as we pray. We need to continue to ask and thank God for His answers until we experience an answer to our prayers. God may answer, "yes," "no," or "wait."

It amazes me how God will answer almost any prayer that a new Christian prays. When babies are born into a family, they get constant attention every time they cry. When they begin to grow up and mature, they do not always get their own way. As we begin to grow in the Lord, we may not always get our prayers answered the same way. The Lord wants to give us what is best for us, not always what we want.

God instructs us to refuse anxiety as we talk to Him and to walk with Him in a constant attitude of thanksgiving. Philippians 4:6 tells us that we should *"not be anxious about anything, but in everything, by prayer and petition, with thanksgiving, present your requests to God."*

Several years ago, my family had a financial need. We were living on a very small budget and obeying God in every way that we knew. One day, I was praying for the Lord to provide for us financially. I opened the door of our home so that I could go to work, and I saw the most amazing phenomenon. Money was lying all over the place! It was on the front lawn, the porch, and all around the house—even on the back lawn. You may ask, "How did it get there?" I have no idea. Did it ever happen again? No, but I will never forget it. All I know is that God did it, and it was a blessing to us. God is a supernatural God who answers prayers in a supernatural way.

PRAISE AND WORSHIP

Fellowship with God not only includes meditating on His Word and praying but also *worshiping and praising* the Lord. To *praise* God means *to respond to God for what He has done.* Praise God for specific things that He has done in your life.

Worship focuses more on *who God is*—on His person. We thank Him because He is God. Everyone worships something. Some people worship themselves. Some people worship their jobs, a motorcycle, sports, or a spouse. We have been chosen to worship only God. The word *worship* comes from an old Anglo-Saxon word, *weorthscipe*, which means "worthiness, respect."[2] Only God is worthy of glory and praise. The Bible says in John 4:23-24 that we must worship with our hearts; it cannot be merely form because *"...true worshipers will worship the Father in spirit and truth, for they are the kind of worshipers the Father seeks. God is spirit, and His worshipers must worship in spirit and in truth."*

I must admit, I don't always feel like worshiping God. Praising or worshiping the Lord is not to be dependent upon our emotions, but instead on a *decision* that we make. God is worthy of all glory and praise. The Bible says that we should offer Him a sacrifice of praise: *"Through Jesus, therefore, let us continually offer to God a sacrifice of praise—the fruit of lips that confess His name"* (Heb. 13:15).

The tabernacle of David in the Old Testament was known as a place of freedom in praise and worship. Music was so important in

David's day that he appointed people with instruments to praise and worship the Lord (see 1 Chron. 15:16; 16:5-6). God is going to rebuild the tabernacle of David again in the last days (see Acts 15:16) by restoring unbridled praise and worship to His Church.

We need to be involved privately in praise and worship to our God in our times alone with Him. In the same way that the moon reflects the glory of the sun, we will reflect the glory of God in our lives as we spend time worshiping Him. The Book of Psalms is filled with songs of praise to our God. I encourage you to sing those psalms and make up your own songs to give worship to God.

WORTHY TO RECEIVE PRAISE

Heaven is a place that will be filled with praise and worship! Revelation 5:11-12 describes a scene of Heaven:

Then I looked and heard the voice of many angels....They encircled the throne and the living creatures and the elders. In a loud voice they sang: "Worthy is the Lamb, who was slain, to receive power and wealth and wisdom and strength and honor and glory and praise!"

Some people think that worship should be quiet. There is a place for quietly worshiping God, but the Bible also encourages us to worship God with a loud voice (see Ps. 47:1). You can go to a football game and see thousands of people get emotionally charged by a little pigskin being thrown around a field. Think about how much more exciting it is that Jesus Christ went to the cross and gave His life for you! That's why we shout unto God and praise and bless Him—He is worthy to receive the praise due only to Him!

We worship God here on earth in preparation for Heaven. I certainly do not want to be a spiritually dead person who cannot praise the Lord: *"It is not the dead who praise the Lord, those who go down to silence"* (Ps. 115:17).

Although I am not an exceptionally emotional person, when I realize what Jesus Christ did for me, my spirit, soul, and body begin to get caught up in praise and worship to my God. According to the Scripture, the demons of hell can be bound (tied up spiritually) through praise and worship to our God. Psalm 149:6-8 says:

May the praise of God be in their mouths and a double-edged sword in their hands, to inflict vengeance on the nations and punishment on the peoples, to bind their kings with fetters, their nobles with shackles of iron.

Whether we are alone or with two or three others or with one thousand people, the demons tremble when God's people commune with Him through praise and worship.

God inhabits, actually lives in, the praises of His people: *"But You are holy, enthroned in the praises of Israel"* (Ps. 22:3 NKJV).

EXPRESSING WORSHIP

There are many ways that we can express worship and praise to our God. Here are just a few of the ways mentioned in the Scriptures. First of all, we can kneel before the Lord: *"Come, let us bow down in worship, let us kneel before the Lord our Maker"* (Ps. 95:6).

We can stand and worship our God like the multitude of people in Revelation 7:9-10:

> *...A great multitude that no one could count, from every nation, tribe, people and language, standing before the throne and in front of the Lamb. They were wearing white robes and were holding palm branches in their hands. And they cried out in a loud voice: "Salvation belongs to our God, who sits on the throne, and to the Lamb."*

The Scripture also says that there are times when God calls us to lift up our hands to the Lord: *"I want men everywhere to lift up holy hands in prayer..."* (1 Tim. 2:8).

Other Scriptures teach us that we should be still before the Lord: *"Be still, and know that I am God..."* (Ps. 46:10).

We are also exhorted to praise Him with instruments: *"Praise Him with the sounding of the trumpet, praise Him with the harp and lyre...praise Him with the clash of cymbals, praise Him with resounding cymbals"* (Ps. 150:3,5).

We can also worship the Lord in dance. The word *dance* in Hebrew means *the lifting of the feet.*[3] David danced before the Lord in the Old Testament (see 2 Sam. 6:14). The devil has taken the dance and made it sensual, but God is restoring dance to His Church in purity through praise and worship to our King Jesus. Psalm 149:3 says, *"Let them praise His name with dancing and make music to Him with tambourine and harp."*

God has also called us to sing new songs to our God. Singing a new song is simply asking God to give us a tune or a melody and then allowing the Holy Spirit to give us the words. Or we can take the words directly from the Scriptures and sing them to Him: *"Praise the Lord. Sing to the Lord a new song, His praise in the assembly of the saints"* (Ps. 149:1).

The Scripture also speaks of clapping and shouting unto the Lord. Remember the time when God's people marched around Jericho day after day? On the seventh day, the walls came tumbling down (see Josh. 6). Demons tremble when we shout because of what Jesus Christ has done and because of who He is. The Bible says that we should clap and shout with cries of joy: "*Clap your hands, all you nations; shout to God with cries of joy*" (Ps. 47:1).

Living a life of praise and worship to our God is so much more than singing a hymn or the most recent worship song. Whenever we choose to live in obedience to the Lord, this is an act of worship (see Rom. 12:1-2). Living a life of thanksgiving tells Him that we believe that He is with us and that He is in control of the outcome of all of our circumstances. It releases the presence of God in our lives.

Ephesians 5:19 says that we should be speaking to one another in psalms and hymns and spiritual songs and making melody in our hearts to the Lord. When a couple gets married, the greatest desire that they have is to be in a relationship together, to spend time together. This involves both speaking and listening. Our God wants us to have communion and relationship with Him. Sometimes we express that relationship by being quiet and listening. Sometimes we shout unto our God. Other times we talk or weep. We've been created to praise and commune with our wonderful, heavenly Daddy.

ENDNOTES

1. Larry Kreider, *Building Your Personal House of Prayer* (Shippensburg, PA: Destiny Image Publishers, 2008); www.h2hp.com.

2. *Merriam-Webster's Collegiate Dictionary*, 11th ed., s.v. "Worship."

3. W. E. Vine, *Vine's Expository Dictionary of Old and New Testament Words*, (Old Tappan, NJ: Fleming H. Revell Company, 1981), s.v. "Dance."

KNOWING GOD THROUGH PRAYER AND WORSHIP
REFLECTION QUESTIONS

1. Describe prayer in your own words.

2. How can we eliminate anxiety from our lives, according to Philippians 4:6?

3. How does God live in our praises?

4. List the physical ways that we can express our worship to God. How many do you use when worshiping God?

Chapter 3

HOW CAN WE HEAR GOD'S VOICE?

"IS THAT YOU, GOD?"

One evening after I taught at a church, a young man came to me and shared his struggle. "I feel the Lord is calling me to go to the mission field, but I'm not sure if I should quit my job or not. I keep hearing different voices. How do I know whether or not I am hearing God's voice clearly?"

Another time, a young man in his late teens stopped by our house and declared that he had heard God's voice. He had a strange expression on his face and then spelled it out. "The Lord spoke to me today...and He told me to kill myself." I was momentarily stunned! But I knew from the Word of God that the Lord would never tell someone to kill himself. It was clear the young man was hearing some other voice.

One time I was driving down a rural road when I passed a hitch-hiker. I sensed a voice telling me to go back and pick him up. I thought the Lord wanted me to share my faith with him. When I turned around, he was nowhere in sight. I was confused. I thought the Lord had spoken to me.

Christians sometimes find themselves in situations where they struggle to hear God's voice. We really want to do what the Lord wants us to do. We know that we serve a living God who wants to speak to us, and yet we struggle with the fact that we often do not hear as clearly as we would like to. Sometimes we may think we have heard the Lord's voice and respond to it, only to find out that we were wrong. Instead of pressing in to find out why we "missed it," we hesitate to step out in faith the next time. Other times, we get so involved in the affairs of this natural world that we forget to listen to the voice of the Lord and receive His instructions for our daily living.

You probably know this already, but the Lord does not speak to us in reverb. Granted, in the classic movie, *The Ten Commandments*, the Lord spoke to Moses in a deep, booming voice, but that was only sound effects! How does He really speak to us? How can we hear His voice?

Let's see what God's Word says about hearing His voice. One day, Jesus made an interesting statement, *"The one who sent Me is with Me; He has not left Me alone, for I always do what pleases Him"* (John 8:29).

Jesus does only what the Father in Heaven has told Him to do. If it is important for Jesus to hear from His Father in Heaven, how much more important is it for each of us to hear His voice clearly? Read on to discover how to hear God's voice more clearly.

ACKNOWLEDGE GOD'S VOICE

For those who are willing to check in with their heavenly Father about decisions of life, Proverbs 3:5-6 promises, *"Trust in the Lord with all your heart and lean not on your own understanding; in all your ways acknowledge Him, and He will make your paths straight."*

After serving the Lord for nearly four decades, I am totally convinced that it is a whole lot harder to get out of His will than we think. If we do get off course, He will reach out in love and nudge us back on track, if we are really trusting and acknowledging Him in our lives.

What does *acknowledge* mean? *Merriam-Webster's Dictionary* says it is "to recognize the rights, status, or authority of; to express gratitude or obligation for; to recognize as genuine or valid."[1] So then, if we acknowledge a new friend, we talk to him, express our appreciation for him, and recognize his presence in our lives.

Imagine your friends not acknowledging your presence when you are together. You try to talk to them, and they completely ignore you. In fact, they talk right over you as if you were not even there. That is how we treat the Lord if we are not acknowledging Him moment by moment in our lives. If we are not recognizing His presence in our lives, we are probably not hearing the voice of the Lord as we should.

The Lord desires to speak to us in many ways, and we need to allow Him to do so. I spend much of my time traveling throughout the world teaching the Bible. One of the things that I miss most when I travel is communicating with my family. I really miss spending time with my wife, LaVerne. However, because of the technologically advanced age we live in, I can usually communicate with her regardless of where I am in the world. I don't care whether the message comes by phone, fax, e-mail, letter, or a note. I just want to hear from her.

We need to get to a place where we want to hear God's voice desperately. This desire comes out of a love relationship with Him. There are many, many ways that God speaks to us. Let's not get too selective about how the Lord speaks to us. In my book *Speak Lord, I'm Listening: How to Hear God's Voice Above the Noise,*[2] I cover 50 ways that God speaks, and the list is not exhaustive!

The Lord may speak to us through others, His peace, circumstances, conviction, dreams, visions, and many other ways. Usually, however, the Lord speaks to us either by His Word or by His Spirit speaking to our spirits. Jesus tells us that if we continue in His Word, we shall know the truth: *"...If you hold to My teaching, you are really My disciples. Then you will know the truth, and the truth will set you free"* (John 8:31-32). He speaks to us by His Word. We will never go off track if we obey the Word of God.

COMPATIBLE WITH GOD'S WORD

We need to saturate ourselves with God's Word. We must have a full reservoir of the Word of God to draw from so that we do not become deceived by the enemy. Any dream, prophecy, vision, or audible voice that does not line up with Scripture is not the voice of God. Scripture is given as a standard so that we will never get off track. Second Timothy 3:16-17 describes God's Word this way:

All Scripture is God-breathed and is useful for teaching, rebuking, correcting and training in righteousness, so that the man of God may be thoroughly equipped for every good work.

A man asked me one time if I could give my "stamp of approval" on his decision to divorce his wife and marry another woman in the church whom he felt could be more compatible with him in his ministry. I told him that, no matter how right it felt to him, his plan was in direct disobedience to the Lord. How did I know? I knew from the Scriptures, in Mark 10:11-12, that he would be committing adultery.

If we want to mature in our Christian lives, we will learn to renew our minds with God's Word so that we can distinguish between good and evil. We will practice doing right: *"You will never be able to eat solid spiritual food and understand the deeper things of God's Word until you become better Christians and learn right from wrong by practicing doing right"* (Heb. 5:14 TLB).

God's Word never changes. Many times, however, the area in which we need guidance is not in direct conflict with the Scriptures. We may need to know the answers for some of the following questions: What is the Lord's plan for my career? Do I need to consider further training? Where should I live? Should I buy a house or a car? Where should I go to college? With which group of believers has the Lord called me to serve? This is the time to learn to listen to the voice of the Holy Spirit speaking to our spirits.

LET HIM ENLIGHTEN YOUR SPIRIT

The Lord desires to speak to us by His Spirit. Romans 8:16 says, *"The Spirit Himself testifies with our spirit that we are God's children."* Proverbs 20:27 says, *"The lamp of the Lord searches the spirit of a man; it searches out his inmost being."*

Your spirit, along with your soul, dwells inside your body. Your spirit and soul live forever. Your soul includes your mind, will, and emotions, and your spirit communicates with the Holy Spirit.

We are learning on this earth how we can communicate with the Holy Spirit. Many times, we hear a voice deep within us but excuse it as "just us." The Lord wants to teach us to trust the Holy Spirit to speak to our spirit. Our spirit is like a lamp that the Lord will "light" and use to give us clear direction.

We often think that hearing God's voice is complicated. It is really not as hard as we think. When my wife and I were preparing to become missionaries as a young couple, we had two choices. Our mission board told us that there were openings in the states of Connecticut and South Carolina. As we prayed, the Lord placed a burden on our hearts for the people on an island off the coast of South Carolina. We didn't hear God speak in an audible voice, but the feeling kept getting stronger. We knew that it was the right place.

We need to expect an answer from the Lord when we are really serious about listening to Him. The Scriptures tell us, *"In his heart a man plans his course, but the Lord determines his steps"* (Prov. 16:9). Look back at your life and see how the Lord has directed your steps. Sometimes God speaks to us by putting a desire or burden in our hearts that we know would not be from anyone else but God.

You can trust God. He speaks to those whose trust is completely in Him. As a boy growing up, I trapped muskrats every winter. Early every morning, before dawn, I would follow the trap line to inspect my traps. Whenever I saw moving shadows or heard strange sounds, I would freeze in my tracks with fear. On those dark, cold, wintery mornings, the most comforting sound I could hear was the voice of my father, who would finish his morning chores and meet me on the trap line. Just the sound of his voice calling my name gave me a sense of peace and security.

Jesus is teaching us to hear His voice. He tells us, in John 10:4, that the sheep hear the shepherd's voice: *"When he has brought out all his own, he goes on ahead of them, and his sheep follow him because they know his voice."* There are various voices that the sheep hear; however, they will not follow the voice of a stranger. The sheep have been trained to only follow the voice of the shepherd.

FOUR DIFFERENT VOICES

When I first became a Christian, I thought that, from that day on, I was only going to hear the voice of God. Wow, was I ever in for a shock! I actually heard all kinds of voices inside my head. I soon realized that some of those voices most certainly were not the voice of the Holy Spirit. As time went on, experience taught me that there are at least four different kinds of voices a person may hear. If we are not hearing God's voice, we are hearing our own voice, the voice of others, or even the devil's voice at times. How can we know which voice is resounding inside of us?

OUR OWN VOICE

Let's talk about our own voice first. Remember, our soul is our mind, will, and emotions. Often, the decisions that we want to make originate from our beliefs, which are manifested in our feelings and emotions. This includes our personal preferences and desires, such as whether or not we like pizza, who our favorite football team is, or if we like shopping, deer hunting, or cherry pie. These things are not wrong, but they are personal preferences, not the voice of God. Many times, Christians confuse their own desires with the voice of the Lord.

OTHER PEOPLE'S VOICES

Instead of God's voice, we may also hear other people's voices vying for our attention. Second Corinthians 10:5 tells us, *"We demolish arguments and every pretension that sets itself up against the knowledge of God, and we take captive every thought to make it obedient to Christ."*

Many times, the voices that we hear have been placed inside of us by those who try to sell us their products or philosophies. Whenever these thoughts and opinions are hostile to the Word of God, we are told to demolish them.

Sometimes it is difficult to know if we have heard from God correctly and to know if others have also heard correctly. We are told in First John 4:1 to test the "spirits." If another believer speaks out a "word from God" for you, test it. Ask God to confirm to you if this is really from Him. If you have any doubts, go to your pastor or other Christian leader. Ask them to pray about it with you.

THE VOICE OF THE ENEMY

A third voice that we may hear instead of God's voice is the voice of the enemy. The devil does not appear to us in a red jumpsuit with a long tail. He comes very slyly as an angel of light (see 2 Cor. 11:14). He may use well-meaning people to speak words that could water down our faith. Or, he could place thoughts into our minds that are contrary to God's Word.

How often have you decided to get serious about studying the Scriptures, and a voice informs you that there are chores that need to be completed immediately? Tell the devil the same thing that Jesus told him, "It is written." Resist him in Jesus' name, and he will flee! (See James 4:7.)

For a time in my life, the enemy would attempt to place a cloud of depression around me. One day, I boldly spoke the Word to myself and the powers of darkness. I shouted, *"...the One who is in* [me] *is greater than the one who is in the world"* (1 John 4:4).

Within minutes, the whole atmosphere changed. The presence of the Lord replaced the presence of the enemy. I had silenced the enemy's voice by proclaiming the truth of the Word of God.

THE VOICE OF GOD

The real voice we want to hear and obey is the voice of our God speaking to our spirit. We often call the Lord's voice a "still, small voice." This phrase comes from the story of Elijah in First Kings 19:11-13, when God spoke to him in a "still, small voice." Often, we are looking for the Lord to speak to us in an earth-shattering way. But the Lord usually speaks to us by His Spirit, deep within our spirits.

Psalm 46:10 says, *"Be still, and know that I am God...."* It is important to take time to be quiet and listen. If you get together with a close friend and do all the talking without listening, the relationship is one-sided. In our prayers, we should talk to God, but we need to listen, too.

Most of the major decisions in my life have come as a result of that "still, small voice." When the Lord spoke to me many years ago about planting a new church through small groups, He asked, "Are you willing to be involved in the underground church?" It was not a booming voice in an earthquake, but a "still, small voice." The "voice" was very clear—it changed the direction of my life.

There are times when I am picking up something for my family at the grocery store and a "still, small voice" tells me to purchase an extra item that is not on the list. Nearly always, when I get home, the item that I chose was needed. If we are sensitive to the Holy Spirit, we will hear when He speaks. On one occasion, the Holy Spirit asked me to give some money to a missionary family. I was later informed that they had no money for food and that this gift was an answer to their prayers.

Ask God to communicate to you during your times with Him and all throughout the day. You will learn more and more to discern your own voice from the Holy Spirit's. You will learn how to hear the voice of God and obey Him.

TUNING IN TO GOD'S VOICE

Did you ever experience a verse almost leaping off the pages of the Bible? You may have read it one thousand times, but this time it really "grabs" you. God is speaking to you!

A husband may be relaxing and feel impressed to help his wife with some of the maintenance around the house. He should not be too quick to rebuke that thought! It is probably the Lord speaking to him. A teenager is listening to her favorite CD or talking to one of her friends on the telephone. A voice inside tells her to clean her room. It is probably God.

We learn to hear the voice of the Lord through practice and obedience. Sometimes we may feel discouraged trying to discern between the Lord's voice, the enemy's voice, others' voices, and our own voice. Sometimes it seems like we are listening to a radio station with a weak signal, while a few other stations continue to fade in and out. But, as we continue to listen to the voice of our Shepherd, we will learn the difference between the voices.

Loren Cunningham, the founder of Youth With A Mission, says that he has found three simple steps that have helped him and thousands of YWAMers to hear God's voice:

***Submit* to His Lordship.** Ask Him to help you silence your own thoughts, desires, and the opinions of others which may be filling your mind (see 2 Cor. 10:5). Even though you have been given a good mind to use, you want to hear the thoughts of the Lord who has the best mind (see Prov. 3:5-6).

***Resist* the Enemy** in case he is trying to deceive you. Use the authority that Jesus Christ has given you to silence the voice of the enemy (see James 4:7; Eph. 6:10-20).

***Expect* an Answer.** After asking the question that is on your mind, wait for Him to answer. Expect your loving heavenly Father to speak to you, and He will (see John 10:27; Ps. 69:13; Exod. 33:11).

Years ago, we were at a shopping mall with our two younger children. In one split second, our then four-year-old daughter was missing from view. I instantly called out her name. Thankfully, she quickly responded to the voice of her father. I was so relieved to see her! Our heavenly Father wants His children to heed His voice. *Lord, teach us to hear Your voice and to obey it.*

ENDNOTES

1. *Merriam-Webster's Collegiate Dictionary*, 11ᵗʰ ed., s.v. "Acknowledge."

2. Larry Kreider, *Speak Lord, I'm Listening: How to Hear God's Voice Above the Noise* (Ventura, CA: Regal Books, 2008); www.h2hp.com.

HOW CAN WE HEAR GOD'S VOICE?
REFLECTION QUESTIONS

1. Have you ever obeyed what you thought was God's voice and later found it was not? Explain.

2. What is the first step in determining if some thought or word is from God (see 2 Tim. 3:16-17)?

3. What are some ways that the Lord has spoken to you through the Holy Spirit?

4. Name some ways that you resist the devil and his lies.

Chapter 4

HEARING
HIS VOICE CLEARLY

THE STRUGGLE TO STAY ON TRACK

Sometimes hearing the voice of the Lord is like driving down the road through intense fog late at night. It is really a struggle. The painted line in the center is our guide, and if we can see a car in front of us, we can follow its taillights. The painted line in the center of the road is symbolic of the Word of God. The most basic way that God speaks is through His Word, and we cannot go wrong by following it. The taillights from the car that we are following are symbolic of the Holy Spirit who guides us and helps us to stay on track.

There are times, however, when it seems like we have entirely lost our way. We really want to obey the Lord and fulfill His will for our lives, but somehow we can no longer see the taillights of the car in front of us or the painted line on the road. What do we do then? There is a story in the Old Testament that gives us some insight. A man was cutting down a tree by the river when his iron axhead fell into the water. An axhead was a very expensive tool, and the man desperately wanted to retrieve it because it was borrowed. He went to Elisha, a man of God, for help. Elisha asked where he had last seen it fall, threw a stick in the water, and it miraculously floated to the surface (see 2 Kings 6:1-6). At the same place that it was lost, the axhead reappeared!

We can learn an important lesson from this. Whenever we have problems with finding direction in our lives, it is often helpful to go back to where we were certain we last heard the voice of the Lord clearly. If we do not go back, we may continue to flounder and be distressed. If we believe that we've lost our way spiritually, the Bible is very clear: *"...Remember the height from which you have fallen! Repent and do the things you did at first..."* (Rev. 2:5).

We must go back to where the axhead fell and remember the height from which we have fallen—where our love and obedience for the Lord declined. We need to acknowledge the Lord when we get off track, repent (turn around), and go back to the last time that we heard the clear, sharp, cutting-edge voice of the Lord. Then obey.

I once read about a young man whom the Lord called to go far from home to a Bible school. After spending a few weeks in the school, he found himself having second thoughts about his decision. He hated the discipline, the climate—you name it. He stayed, however, when he remembered the time that the Lord had clearly called him to go to that school. By being obedient, he was a recipient of the benefits, and the Lord did a tremendous work in His life.

GO BACK

In 1992, I began to question whether or not I was called to church leadership. Anything else looked much better than to continue on in a leadership role. However, I remembered the initial call when God called me to start a new church in 1980. This was the place the axhead had fallen for me, and I was convinced that the Lord had spoken to me and given me a mandate to start the church. Knowing this gave me the confidence to go on. I knew that He had not yet completed the work He had begun.

Do you get tired of your job sometimes? Perhaps you are tired of going to school or of your involvement in the Church. Go back to the last time that you know you heard clearly from the Lord on the subject, and allow the Lord to take you from there. If you made a mistake, there is hope. That is why Jesus came in the first place, to forgive us as we acknowledge our sin, to cleanse us, and to give us a brand-new start.

Remember Jonah? He refused to obey the Lord, who told him to preach the Gospel in the city of Nineveh. God got his attention by using ungodly sailors to push him into the ocean, and the Lord prepared a great fish to swallow him alive to give him some time to think. I believe Jonah thought back to where "the axhead fell" (he went off-track) and quickly repented! The Lord gave him another chance, and the fish spit him out on dry land. The Bible says in Jonah 3:1, *"Then the word of the Lord came to Jonah a second time: 'Go to the great city of Nineveh and proclaim to it the message I give you.' Jonah obeyed the word of the Lord and went to Nineveh"* (Jon. 3:1-3a).

As we repent before God, we can receive the word of the Lord a second time. A key question to ask ourselves is this, "Have I obeyed the last thing that the Lord asked me to do?"

One thing that used to cause stress in our marriage was the fact that I was constantly trying to find shortcuts whenever my wife, LaVerne, and I were driving somewhere. To make matters worse, I usually got lost! To backtrack over and over again was embarrassing! I usually needed to go back to the last road that I was familiar with before I could find the way.

If you find yourself on the wrong path, it is not the end of the world. The Lord is able to *"restore the years that the locusts have* eaten" (see Joel 2:25), but going back to the place where we last heard from God is often the way to get to our destination.

GOD'S WORD SHOULD "ALIGN"

I learned a principle from a man of God once that has helped steer me in the right direction as I have attempted to hear God's voice. This man told a story of three lighthouses that were built to warn ships of the monstrous rocks which were below the surface of the water as they sailed into the harbor. To avoid getting snagged on these huge rocks, the captain had to be sure that the three lighthouses were aligned as he sailed into the harbor. If the captain could see two or three lighthouses at the same time, he knew that he was in the danger zone.

In order to avoid shipwreck in our lives, we need to be sure that three different "lighthouses" are aligned before we begin to move in a new direction.

The first lighthouse to align is the Word of God. There is no substitute for God's Word. Paul the apostle tells us in First Corinthians 14:37, *"If anyone thinks himself to be a prophet or spiritual, let him acknowledge that the things which I write to you are the commandments of the Lord"* (NKJV). God told Joshua in Joshua 1:8 to be faithful to God's Word: *"Do not let this Book of the Law depart from your mouth; meditate on it day and night, so that you may be careful to do everything written in it. Then you will be prosperous and successful."*

When we obey the Word of God, we are promised success. When we disobey the Word of God, it will cause shipwreck in our lives. Things may be OK for a period of time, but eventually disobedience to God's Word will take a toll on our lives.

If anyone claims to have supernatural revelation from God, it must line up with the Word of God. The whole Mormon cult was started by Joseph Smith, a man who claimed that he had a visitation from an angel. We know that this was really a fallen angel or demonic spiritual being because the message did not line up with the Word of God. It was a perversion of the true Gospel. Paul the apostle urges the Galatian believers to not be persuaded by false teachers in Galatians 1:6-8:

> *I am astonished that you are so quickly deserting the one who called you by the grace of Christ and are turning to a different gospel—which is really no gospel at all. Evidently some people are throwing you into confusion and are trying to pervert the gospel of Christ. But even if we or an angel from heaven should preach a gospel other than the one we preached to you, let him be eternally condemned!*

Remember, the Bible says that satan comes to us like an angel of light (see 2 Cor. 11:14). Check everything against the Word of God. If you are not sure, go to a mature believer or leader of your church. The Word of God is our standard to be sure that the revelation that we are getting is in line with the perfect will of God.

GOD'S PEACE SHOULD "ALIGN"

The second spiritual lighthouse that needs to line up is the peace of God. The Scriptures tell us in Colossians 3:15, *"Let the peace of Christ rule in your hearts, since as members of one body you were called to peace. And be thankful."* The word *rule* literally means "to act as an umpire."[1] In other words, the peace of God in our hearts is an umpire to alert us as to whether or not we should make a certain decision.

A man was offered a job by a large company where he would make much more money than he ever made in his life. He thought of all the wonderful things that he could do with the money—use it to help friends who needed to buy an apartment, give money to the poor, help the homeless. However, he did not have peace from God about taking the job, so he turned it down. The president of the company thought he was crazy, as did some friends. It seemed like a once-in-a-lifetime opportunity. But he could not take it without the blessing of God. A short time later, he found out that the president of the company had done many illegal things and that the whole company was in trouble. If he had taken the job, he might have been implicated just because he worked there. At the very least, he would have had to choose between being honest and keeping the job. God kept this man from getting involved in a very chaotic situation.

Several years ago, a friend told me that he wanted to give me his car. It was a beautiful car, but my wife, LaVerne, and I did not have the peace of God in our hearts to receive it. So we graciously declined. Some time later, the Lord provided our family with a van, and this time we had the peace to receive it from the benefactor. Obeying the peace of God in our hearts allows us to carry on with a sense of His acceptance and favor in our lives.

CIRCUMSTANCES SHOULD "ALIGN"

The third lighthouse to align is *circumstances*. Sometimes we can be so sure that something is God's will but that it is not the right timing for us. If you feel this way, it is best to let the desire die. If it is really from God, He will resurrect it (bring it back to life) in the future when the timing is right.

We have counseled countless young men and women who were sure that the Lord had shown them whom they should marry, but the other person wasn't getting the same message. Our advice was to let the desire die and trust that, if the Lord has really spoken it to them, it will happen sometime in the future.

If you believe the Lord wants you to buy a certain house or car, and it is not available, either you have missed the timing, or it is not the Lord's answer for you. Timing is so important. You may have the right *direction* from the Lord but the wrong *timing* as you try to fulfill it. Moses had the right vision from the Lord—deliver the Lord's people from the slavery of the Egyptians. The only problem: he initially missed the timing of God (by 40 years!) when he killed an Egyptian. Someone may feel called to start a business or be a missionary, and the vision is a genuine vision from the Lord. Often the problem comes when he or she jumps into it too fast. When the Lord is in it, the circumstances will work out.

The Lord clearly opened up a door for Paul in First Corinthians 16:8-9. The circumstances lined up with the Word of God and with the peace of God. Although Paul faced many adversaries, he knew that the Lord had opened up the door for him: *"But I will stay on at Ephesus until Pentecost, because a great door for effective work has opened to me, and there are many who oppose me."*

Jeremiah gives an interesting account of heeding the voice of the Lord through circumstances:

Then this message from the Lord came to Jeremiah: "Your cousin Hanamel (son of Shallum) will soon arrive to ask you to buy the farm he owns in Anathoth, for by law you have a chance to buy before it is offered to anyone else." So, Hanamel came, as the Lord had said he would, and visited me in the prison. "Buy my field in Anathoth, in the land of Benjamin," he said, "for the law gives you the first right to purchase it." Then I knew for sure that the message I had heard was really from the Lord (Jeremiah 32:6-8 TLB).

After the circumstances lined up, Jeremiah knew that the message was from the Lord. If the Lord is asking you to do something, He will make it clear. You can trust Him.

GOD WILL MAKE IT CLEAR

George Müller was a man of faith from Bristol, England, who fed hundreds of children in his orphanages in 19th-century England. The following relates his valuable insights on hearing from God:

I seek at the beginning to get my heart in such a state that it has no will of its own in regard to a given matter. Nine-tenths of the trouble with people generally is just there. Nine-tenths of the difficulties are overcome when our hearts are ready to do the Lord's will whatever it may be. When one is truly in this state, it is usually but a little way to the knowledge of what His will is.

Having done this, I do not leave the result to feeling or simple impression. If so, I make myself liable to great delusions.

I will seek the will of the Spirit of God through, or in connection with, the Word of God. The Spirit and the Word must be combined. If I look to the Spirit alone without the Word,

I lay myself open to great delusions also. If the Holy Ghost guides us at all, He will do it according to the Scriptures and never contrary to them.

Next, I take into account providential circumstances. These often plainly indicate God's will in connection with His Word and Spirit.

I ask God in prayer to reveal His will to me aright.

Thus, through prayer to God, the study of the Word, and reflection, I come to deliberate judgment according to the best of my ability and knowledge, and if my mind is thus at peace, and continues so after two or three more petitions, I proceed accordingly. In trivial matters and in transactions involving most important issues, I find this method always effective.[2]

I never remember, in all of my Christian course, a period now (in March 1895) of sixty-nine years and four months, that I ever sincerely and patiently sought to know the will of God by the teaching of the Holy Ghost, through the instrumentality of the Word of God, but I have always been directed rightly. But if honesty of heart and uprightness before God were lacking, or if I did not patiently wait upon God for instruction, or if I preferred the counsel of my fellow man to the declarations of the Word of the living God, I made great mistakes.[3]

That is good advice. Let us look for the three lighthouse beacon lights (the Word of God, the peace of God, and circumstances) to line up in the days ahead. If the lights do not line up, we are in danger of running into the rocks. I'm heading for the three beacon lights. How about you?

LISTEN AND COMMUNICATE

My wife, LaVerne, learned years ago the importance of communing with God and having a real love relationship with her Father in Heaven. Sometime back, she shared these thoughts with a group of believers:

> We as a Church are engaged to Jesus, the Bridegroom who is coming back for us—the Bride. What do engaged couples do to have an effective relationship? They spend time together, not just talking, but listening to each other's hearts, sharing each other's dreams. As they listen and talk together, they understand each other. If they just talk and do not listen, they have an ineffective relationship. So it is in our relationship with Jesus. It is Jesus' desire that we listen to Him and commune with Him. We need to see that we are engaged to Him, and the Word of God needs to be powerful in our lives. When the Word of God is in us, we understand and know who God is. We understand that He wants to speak to us. The Word of God is spirit and life within us. As we drive down the road, as we wash dishes, as we sit at the desk, we are aware of His presence and are willing to listen to that "still, small voice" based on the Word of God because the Word of God is in us. God desires to speak to us all day long. It is up to us to listen to Him.

Just as a husband and wife learn to communicate and have fellowship with one another and grow in their love relationship, the Lord teaches us to grow in our love relationship with Him. Jesus, our Bridegroom, is coming back for us. Nothing is more important or has more eternal significance:

> *Husbands, love your wives, just as Christ loved the church and gave Himself up for her to make her holy, cleansing her by the washing with water through the word, and to present her to Himself as a radiant church, without stain or wrinkle or any other blemish, but holy and blameless* (Ephesians 5:25-27).

Jesus gave His life for us on the cross two thousand years ago. He paid the price for us to experience a loving relationship with our heavenly Father. He desires to guide and lead us as we build a relationship with Him. He is worthy of our fellowship and of our worship.

ENDNOTES

1. W. E. Vine, *Vine's Expository Dictionary of Old and New Testament Words*, (Old Tappan, NJ: Fleming H. Revell Company, 1981), s.v. "Rule."

2. George Müller, quoted in A.E.C. Brooks, *Answers to Prayer from George Müller's Narratives* (Chicago, IL: Moody Press, 1970).

3. George Müller, quoted in A.T. Pierson, *George Müller of Bristol* (Grand Rapids, MI: Kregel Publications, 1999).

HEARING HIS VOICE CLEARLY
REFLECTION QUESTIONS

1. Give examples of "axheads" in your Christian walk.

2. Have you had an experience where you struggled to repent, like Jonah? What did you do? What should you have done?

3. How does the "peace of God" feel, and how does it affect your life?

4. Describe a situation when you had the right direction from the Lord but missed His perfect timing. How did you know?

PART II

What Is the Church?

Chapter 5

THE IMPORTANCE OF THE LOCAL CHURCH

WE NEED EACH OTHER

I once read the story of a young man who had given his life to God; but after a time of disappointment and disillusionment, he began to withdraw from other Christians. The young man's pastor stopped in for a visit one cold, blustery winter evening, and with the wind howling outside, they sat and talked.

After awhile, the wise pastor walked over to the fireplace, and with a pair of prongs picked up a hot coal from the fire, placing it on the bricks in front of the fireplace. He continued to converse with the young man. Then glancing at the ember on the bricks, he said, "Do you see that piece of coal? While it was in the fireplace it burned brightly, but now that it's alone, the ember has almost gone out."

The pastor walked over to the fireplace, and with the prongs, picked up the ember and placed it inside the fireplace. Within minutes, the dying ember was again burning brightly.

It suddenly dawned on the young man what the pastor was trying to tell him. When we move away from the warm and encouraging fires of fellow believers in the Body of Christ, we will eventually cool down spiritually. Joining with others as a community of believers in a local church body helps keep our fires glowing. From that day on, the young man made a decision to join regularly with other believers in a local church in his community. He did not want to take the chance of his fire going out again.

The Bible says in Hebrews 3:13, *"But encourage one another daily, as long as it is called Today, so that none of you may be hardened by sin's deceitfulness."* It is extremely difficult to live the Christian life alone. Believers need to fellowship together and encourage one another daily because otherwise it is easy to become increasingly tolerant of sin in our lives.

An elderly friend of mine once said, "Lone Rangers often get shot out of the saddle." He was referring to the popular U.S. television show in the 1950s called "The Lone Ranger." This lone lawman rode to rid the wild west of outlaws and was often vulnerable to attack. If we try to live our Christian lives alone, without the support of other believers, the devil can easily destroy us spiritually. We need each other. Hebrews 10:24-25 tells us:

And let us consider how we may spur one another on toward love and good deeds. Let us not give up meeting together, as some are in the habit of doing, but let us encourage one another—and all the more as you see the Day approaching.

Jesus Christ is coming back soon. We need to stir one another up to be on fire for our Lord Jesus Christ. Meeting together regularly encourages each of us to hold firmly to Christ. God has a plan for us to assemble together on a regular basis so that we can receive teaching, encouragement, and equipping for the work of ministry. He calls this group of believers the "Church." Let's learn about the importance of being solidly connected to a local church.

THE CHURCH—"CALLED OUT ONES"

What is the *Church*, exactly? The Church is not a building or a meeting or a program. The Church of Jesus Christ is simply *people*. As believers, we are the Church. The word *church* literally means *gathering of the called out ones.*[1] The Church then, is a group of people who have been called out of spiritual darkness into the light of God's Kingdom.

When we come to Christ, we are immediately a part of the universal Church of Christ, which includes every believer who has ever named the name of Christ from every nation of the world. Jesus talks about His universal Church in Matthew 16:18: *"And I tell you that you are Peter, and on this rock I will build my church, and the gates of Hades will not overcome it."* I have had the privilege of traveling to six continents of the world. Everywhere I go, I find believers from completely different backgrounds, with different skin colors and different cultures who have one thing in common. They all have the same heavenly Father, have received Jesus Christ as Lord, and are part of the same family.

One time, while flying in an airplane, the businessman sitting next to me began to tell me about the corporation he represents. Then he asked me, "What do you do?" I told him that I am a part of the largest corporation in the world. "In fact," I said, "we are now in every country of the world." Of course, I was talking about the Kingdom of God—God's wonderful and universal family, the Church of Jesus Christ.

The Bible is talking about the universal Church when it says that all of the saints of the whole Church of God, and all of His children in Heaven and earth will acknowledge that Jesus Christ is alone worthy: *"...with your blood you purchased men for God from every tribe and language and people and nation"* (Rev. 5:9).

Jesus has promised that He will build His Church and that the gates of hell will not prevail against it (see Matt. 16:18). We can be assured that, regardless of what happens in the world today, Jesus Christ is building His Church, and we have the privilege of being a part of it.

But the word *church* also refers to the *local* church. Within God's universal Church family are *local* churches in each community, which provide the support and love each believer needs.

A BABY CHRISTIAN NEEDS A FAMILY

Every believer needs a "support system" to survive. When I have the privilege of leading someone to Christ, I often tell him that he is now a "baby Christian" and needs to understand four important truths of spiritual nourishment. First of all, every baby needs to eat and drink. That's why the Bible says in First Peter 2:2 that baby Christians need to first drink the milk of God's Word so that they can begin to grow: *"Like newborn babies, crave pure spiritual milk, so that by it you may grow up in your salvation."*

Second, to remain alive, every baby needs to breathe. Baby Christians (and mature ones!) breathe spiritually through prayer as we contemplatively and deeply rest in God's presence as we communicate with our Father in Heaven. The Bible tells us to *"pray continually"* (1 Thess. 5:17).

Third, we need to exercise—to share our faith with others. The Scriptures tell us, *"Let the redeemed of the Lord say so..."* (Ps. 107:2 NKJV).

And fourth, baby Christians need to stay warm. We stay warm through being committed to other believers in a local church and having regular fellowship with them. We are a part of a spiritual family—a family of the redeemed who are joined under one Father in Christ: *"For this reason I kneel before the Father, from whom His whole family in heaven and on earth derives its name"* (Eph. 3:14-15).

In the local church, we are part of a spiritual family united under Christ. This spiritual family gives us a place to grow and learn from other believers how to live our Christian lives. We need this input from others.

You will find that there is no perfect local church. However, this is no excuse for not getting involved in a church in our community. If we could find a church that was perfect, the moment we joined, the church would no longer be perfect, because we are not perfect!

Our salvation, of course, does not come through being joined to a local church; it comes by knowing God our Father through a personal relationship with Jesus Christ. When we join to Christ, we become his sons and daughters: *"'I will be a Father to you, and you will be my sons and daughters,' says the Lord Almighty"* (2 Cor. 6:18).

However, once we are children of God, we should want to join other Christians so that we can receive their love and care. As soon as we give our lives to Christ, we should ask the Lord where He desires to place us in His family, which church in our community He would have us join.

THE LOCAL CHURCH IS GOD'S ARMY

We need one another. We are not supposed to live the Christian life alone. The Lord has called us to be a company of spiritual soldiers who serve in His spiritual army: *"Endure hardship with us like a good soldier of Christ Jesus"* (2 Tim. 2:3).

A former military officer once told me that what kept him going in the war more than anything else was the camaraderie that he developed with fellow soldiers. We are in a spiritual war, and we need the support of our fellow Christian soldiers because we are fighting the devil who is out to kill, steal from, and destroy the people of God (see John 10:10).

Armies are made up of small groups called platoons. In the New Testament Church, the believers met from house to house (in small groups) as well as in the temple (in large groups). Meeting in a local church fellowship is especially important because it allows us to be encouraged and trained as spiritual soldiers. It is so important to find the place where God can use us best in His Kingdom.

The local church is not only for training to go into the world. Just as all armies have medical units, the church is also a place we can be cared for, healed, and strengthened when we are weak. It is a place where we can be set free to live transformed, victorious lives so that we can go out to the spiritual battlefield with power. By the power and authority of Jesus Christ, in local churches, people can be set free from besetting sins, life-controlling problems, and bad habits.

Sometimes today, churches look more like social clubs than a spiritual army. People attend meetings for the social interaction and forget their true purpose. God has called His Church to return to its original purpose to be a standard of righteousness in our generation. Isaiah 59:19 says that *"...When the enemy comes in like a flood, the Spirit of the Lord will lift up a standard against him"* (NKJV). The Church of Jesus Christ is a standard that the Lord is raising up against the enemy who wants to destroy this generation. Each of us needs to find our place in God's army, the local church, and do our part.

FITTING TOGETHER

Like a building that is made up of blocks that have been placed on a wall with mortar, as the Church, we are living stones built together through relationships with one another.

As you come to him, the living Stone—rejected by men but chosen by God and precious to Him—you also, like living stones, are being built into a spiritual house to be a holy priesthood, offering spiritual sacrifices acceptable to God through Jesus Christ (see 1 Pet. 2:4-5).

For we are God's fellow workers; you are God's field, you are God's building (1 Corinthians 3:9 NKJV).

In this Scripture, notice that the Lord calls us a "building" and also a "field." Not only are we to be in relationship with other believers, we should know where we fit in our spiritual "field."

Many times when I fly over countries that have beautiful farm lands, I can see various crops growing in distinct fields. Each local church is a distinct field with believers planted there so that they can grow and reproduce within that particular "field." The Lord's desire is for us to reproduce the life of Jesus in others. It all starts when we are committed to Jesus and to a local church where we can receive help to grow in Christ and help others to grow in the Lord.

That's why it is so important for the local church to be made up of small groups of believers who meet together. It is impossible for a believer to be touching (relating to) dozens or hundreds of people, but in smaller groups we can practically touch a few people. In some churches, these may be called Sunday School classes or Bible study groups. Other churches may use the term home fellowships or cell groups or house churches.

Kelly, a young divorced mother of two, learned just how valuable the relationships she had with those in her small group were. She had let the insurance lapse on her car and then had an accident, causing her driver's license to be suspended for three months. She wondered how she would care for her children because she would lose her job as a school bus driver. Her small group rallied around her in prayer and practical help. During her three months without a job, she had a ride whenever she needed one. Bags of groceries appeared at her doorstep. Kelly learned that God provides through the people whom she was "built together with."

Jesus had a small group of 12 disciples. Moses was commanded by the Lord to break the Israelites down into groups of ten (see Exod. 18). We all have a need for relationship—getting to know others who can provide mutual support as we learn to grow in God and fulfill His purposes in our lives. This best happens in smaller groups with everyone working toward a common goal.

LEADERSHIP AND PROTECTION

Why, you may ask, is it so important to be involved in a local church? For one thing, the local church provides leaders to equip us in our Christian walk. The early Church was encouraged to appoint elders in every city (local church): *"The reason I left you in Crete was that you might straighten out what was left unfinished and appoint elders in every town, as I directed you"* (Titus 1:5).

One of the Lord's purposes for the local church is to provide eldership or spiritual leadership who can equip us, encourage us, and serve us as "undershepherds" under Jesus (who is the Chief Shepherd). These leaders have clear instructions as to what their role is:

> *And we urge you, brothers, warn those who are idle, encourage the timid, help the weak, be patient with everyone. Make sure that nobody pays back wrong for wrong, but always try to be kind to each other and to everyone else* (1 Thessalonians 5:14-15).

These verses tell us that the Lord provides protection and guidance for His people through leaders in the local church. Leaders are to be people of love and patience as they encourage those they serve. They are there to give guidance and correction in love.

In Matthew 18:15-17, Jesus tells how the local church can provide discipline and restoration to a wayward member:

> *If your brother sins against you, go and show him his fault, just between the two of you. If he listens to you, you have won your brother over. But if he will not listen, take one or two others along, so that "every matter may be established by the testimony of two or three witnesses." If he refuses to listen to them, tell it to the church; and if he refuses to listen even to the church, treat him as you would a pagan or a tax collector.*

If a Christian believer sins against us, Jesus instructs us to confront him one-on-one. If he does not listen, we should go with "two or more" believers and again appeal to him. If he still does not hear us, we should "tell it to the church." This is referring to the local church, because it would be impossible to take it to the universal Church! The local church leaders will help to restore such a person back into fellowship.

Local church leaders have the responsibility to keep watch over us by protecting, directing, correcting, and encouraging us: *"Keep watch over yourselves and all the flock of which the Holy Spirit has made you overseers"* (Acts 20:28a).

VULNERABLE WITHOUT A LOCAL CHURCH

Sometimes, through disillusionment, disappointment, or spiritual pride, believers find themselves uninvolved in a local church. This leaves them very vulnerable. The Bible tells us in First Corinthians 10:13:

> *No temptation has seized you except what is common to man. And God is faithful; He will not let you be tempted beyond what you can bear. But when you are tempted, He will also provide a way out so that you can stand up under it.*

The local church is often "the way out" that the Lord has prepared for His people during an onslaught of the devil. When we fellowship with other believers, we realize that we are not alone in the temptations that we face. We receive spiritual protection, strength, and oversight from the spiritual leaders that the Lord has placed in our lives. The Lord's plan is to use the local church to protect us, help us grow, and equip us to be all that we can be in Jesus Christ.

I heard a story once of an evangelist who had a choir that included singers from many churches in the community in which he was preaching. A lady came to him one day and said, "I would like to sing in your choir." When the evangelist asked her which local church she represented, she said, "I am involved in the universal church."

He said to her, "Then find the pastor of the universal church and sing in his choir." In other words, he was concerned about this lady's noninvolvement in a local church. He recognized the need to be committed to a local church for spiritual protection and accountability.

Spiritual leaders and other believers in the local church are there to exhort you, comfort you, and uphold you in prayer.

ENDNOTE

1. Joseph Thayer, *Thayer's Greek-English Lexicon of the New Testament*, s.v. "Church."

THE IMPORTANCE OF THE LOCAL CHURCH
REFLECTION QUESTIONS

1. What are the four things that a spiritual baby needs in order to grow spiritually?

2. How are you God's field and building (see 1 Cor. 3:9)?

3. Do you know where you fit into God's Kingdom?

4. What are some things that spiritual leaders provide in the local church (see 1 Thess. 5:14-15)?

Chapter 6

SPIRITUAL FAMILY RELATIONSHIPS

CHURCH AS FAMILY

Many young couples who get married are in for a big surprise. They thought that they were only marrying one person, but they realize after the wedding that they married into an entire family! They have to get to know grandparents, uncles and aunts, cousins, dad and mom, and all of the rest of the in-laws. In the family of God, when you and I make a decision to become a part of a local church, we become a part of an entire church family. Galatians 3:26 tells us that sonship with God involves brotherhood with Jesus. Christians are related as family. We are all brothers and sisters through Jesus: *"You are all sons of God through faith in Christ Jesus"* (Gal 3:26).

In the Old Testament, God's people were always described as part of a larger family. The children of Israel were involved in one of 12 tribes. Each tribe was made up of a group of clans, and each clan was made up of a group of families. Gideon mentions his family, clan, and tribe in Judges 6:15: *"...My clan is the weakest in Manasseh [tribe], and I am the least in my family."* Even today, the Lord continues to see each of us as a part of various spiritual spheres or families.

First, I believe the Lord sees me as an individual believer bought by the blood of Jesus.

He also recognizes that I am a part of a spiritual church family. For me, that spiritual family starts with the small group of believers that I meet with weekly. In small groups, we are nurtured, equipped to serve, and given the opportunity to reach out. Most churches have small groups of believers who meet together—Sunday school classes, youth groups, Bible studies, or fellowships of believers who meet in homes. This kind of small group fellowship is one aspect of a spiritual family.

An additional aspect of spiritual family life happens when whole clusters of small groups relate closely together to form a *congregation* of believers. When I meet on a weekend with my local church congregation, my small group and many others come together to worship and receive the Word of God together. This is an extended spiritual family. According to Romans 16, the believers in Rome met together in homes. It also is clear that they were in relationship with one another throughout the city in extended spiritual family relationships, congregations, or networks of home fellowships.

A third sphere of spiritual family relationships often refers to a church denomination or *family of churches*. Whenever a group of churches work together as a "network of churches" or an "apostolic fellowship," they form a larger sphere of family relationships. Our church is a part of a family of churches which partner together from various parts of the world, representing a larger spiritual family.

The Israelites were made up of 12 tribes and a multitude of clans and families. They were corporately known as "the children of Israel." In the same way, the Church of Jesus Christ is made up of believers in small groups, congregations, and denominations who together represent the Kingdom of God.

FAMILY RELATIONSHIPS BRING UNITY

No matter what our church affiliation or denomination, we become one family through Christ. When we realize that the walls have been broken down and that we need each other as fellow believers in Christ, we will know for sure that every church group in the Body of Christ is important to Him: *"There is neither Jew nor Greek, slave nor free, male nor female, for you are all one in Christ Jesus"* (Gal. 3:28).

Every church in every community and every denomination or family of churches has certain strengths to contribute to help the greater Body of Christ. God uses many different church families to accomplish His purposes here on earth. We are called by the Lord to link arms with other churches, denominations, and groups of believers so that we can with one voice glorify our God and work together to build His Kingdom.

Throughout history, there have been many times when, by His Holy Spirit, God raised up various "movements," new families of churches and denominations to bring reform or refreshment to the Church. For example, many Methodist churches are traced back to the 18th and 19th centuries when John Wesley and the team of men who worked closely with him obeyed the call from the Lord to share the Gospel of Jesus Christ and to "plant" new groups of believers in the nations of the world. Today you can find Methodist church buildings all over the world.

The town I live in has a Moravian church. The Moravians, who have their roots in Europe, were sent to many nations of the world to share the Gospel. In fact, they prayed around the clock 24 hours a day for 100 years as they sent missionaries to the nations of the world to share the Gospel of Jesus Christ and start new churches. They had a real sense of *family* as they labored together.

Throughout the 1960s and '70s, the Charismatic movement literally exploded throughout the world. During that period in Church history, many believers were filled with the Holy Spirit and experienced the gifts of the Holy Spirit. God continues to move among His people today. We are linked together in unity by our spiritual family relationships!

NEW WINESKINS BRING NEW LIFE

I believe the Lord wants to pour out His Spirit in our generation. As He does, thousands of people will come into the Kingdom of God. Jesus tells us to open our eyes and realize there are many lost in the world who need to be saved: *"...I tell you, open your eyes and look at the fields! They are ripe for harvest"* (John 4:35).

But how can these new believers be "harvested?" Traditional, modern-day church structures and programs cannot accommodate a huge harvest. They already have their hands full. I believe we constantly need new churches starting up to provide new wineskins or structures for new believers in Jesus Christ:

> *Neither do men pour new wine into old wineskins. If they do, the skins will burst, the wine will run out and the wineskins will be ruined. No, they pour new wine into new wineskins, and both are preserved* (Matthew 9:17).

A new wineskin is like a balloon—flexible and pliable. Putting a new Christian (new wine) into an old church structure can cause the structure to break, and the new Christian may be lost. New

Christians should be placed in new church structures that are flexible and able to encourage their spiritual growth. Such new "wineskins" may be a small group of believers meeting in a house church or cell group. In small groups, people can be easily nurtured, discipled, and trained as leaders.

I believe the Lord will be raising up many new "wineskins" (new types of churches) to help bring in the harvest. God is preparing laborers to reach the masses with the Gospel of Jesus Christ in our generation. He will require many of us to be involved with new groups of believers (new wineskins) in the future as the Lord calls us to the nations of the world. The newer house church networks[1] and cell groups will work with the more traditional churches already in our neighborhoods today.

We must work together. Sometimes people involved in newer churches have a tendency to look down on churches that have been around awhile. Instead, they should honor their "fathers"—those who have gone before them. And those in older churches should be glad when new movements and churches are started because they help to bring the Gospel of Christ to a dying world.

We need every church body to be involved in planting new churches throughout the nations of the world. Every local church should have a world vision. Jesus instructed His disciples before He ascended into Heaven: *"But you will receive power when the Holy Spirit comes on you; and you will be my witnesses in Jerusalem, and in all Judea and Samaria, and to the ends of the earth"* (Acts 1:8).

In other words, the Lord is calling us as His Church to share the Gospel, make disciples, and start new churches in Jerusalem (our home town), Judea (our region), Samaria (our neighboring state or country), and to the end of the earth (the nations of the world).

MEETING HOUSE TO HOUSE AS A FAMILY

The early Church understood the need for new churches to meet the needs of all of the people coming to the Lord. They met from house to house in small groups and also together in the temple, to receive teaching from the Word of God and to worship the Lord together:

> *Every day they continued to meet together in the temple courts. They broke bread in their homes and ate together with glad and sincere hearts, praising God and enjoying the favor of all the people. And the Lord added to their number daily those who were being saved* (Acts 2:46-47).

After I gave my life to Jesus Christ in 1968, I had a tremendous hunger for God and for His Word. I started meeting with other young believers who were a part of a local church in our community to study the Bible and pray. One day we realized that God had called us to reach the lost around us, yet we were just sitting around enjoying a Bible study. We needed to become fishers of men (see Mark 1:17).

During the next few years, my fiancé and I helped start a youth ministry with a small band of young people who began to reach out to the unchurched youth of our community in Lancaster County, Pennsylvania. We played sports and conducted various activities throughout the week for spiritually needy youngsters and teenagers. This kind of "friendship evangelism" produced results, and during the next few years, dozens of young people came to faith in Christ.

Those of us who served in this youth ministry were from various churches, so we also attempted to help the new believers find their place in our local congregations. Although the Christians in the local churches were friendly and helpful, something still wasn't "clicking." These young believers from unchurched backgrounds were just not being incorporated into the life of the established churches in our communities. We began to realize that there needed to be "new wineskins" for the "new wine."

The Lord clearly spoke to me about starting a new wineskin (new church structure of small groups) for the new wine (new Christians). After receiving the affirmation and blessing of the leadership of the church that had sent us out to start this new work, we stepped out in faith to start a new church in October 1980. Since that time, we've had the privilege of seeing people come to Christ and being built together in local churches throughout six continents of the world.

The Church is people who are built together in a relationship with God and with one another who have been called by God with a common purpose and vision. They serve one another, reach out to those who need Christ, and support the local leadership that God raises up among them.

Real church is much more than going to a meeting every Sunday morning. For example, although we may not think about it often, a healthy tree needs to have a strong root system. In the same way, we have found in the Church that what happens "underground" in small groups, where relationships are built, is of vital importance. When relationships are healthy and strong in small groups, meeting together from house to house, the other church meetings will also be filled with life.

FAMILIES ARE CONNECTED

Can you imagine a builder taking a thousand bricks, throwing them on a big pile, and calling that a building? Ridiculous! In order to build a building, a master planner needs to take hundreds and thousands of bricks and strategically place one upon another and then mortar them together. The mortar that God uses to build His Kingdom is the mortar of relationships. God, the master planner, takes you and me and places us in His Body in strategic places with others so that we can fulfill the Lord's purposes.

Many times we call a building on the street corner the "church," but in reality the true Church is "people." Thank God for buildings that we can use to worship Him and to be taught the Word of God; however, let's never confuse the church building for the true Church, the people of God.

The Bible calls us "living stones." Each believer has been made alive through faith in our Lord Jesus Christ. The Lord builds us together with other Christians into a type of spiritual house or community: *"You also, like living stones, are being built into a spiritual house to be a holy priesthood, offering spiritual sacrifices acceptable to God through Jesus Christ"* (1 Pet. 2:5).

We said before that the term *church* simply means "called-out ones"—those who are called out from the world's system to be a part of God's Kingdom. To be a believer in Jesus Christ is to live counterculture to the world's system of selfishness. We live a new life in a new way, obeying the Word of God.

Jesus Christ lives in His Church, which means that He lives in His people, His called-out ones. Jesus dwells inside us as His people, His Body: *"From Him the whole body, joined and held together by every supporting ligament, grows and builds itself up in love, as each part does its work"* (Eph. 4:16).

Like a human body, our shoulders and arms are linked together by joints and ligaments. These joints and ligaments, spiritually speaking, are relationships in the Body of Christ. Believers joining together in a relationship who realize that Jesus Christ lives in them can supply one another with spiritual strength and life. That's why we need to be connected with other brothers and sisters in the Body of Christ. I need my brothers and sisters to supply what I need to grow spiritually.

WHERE HAS GOD PLACED YOU?

The Lord who has created our bodies tells us that we are like a spiritual body. Aren't you grateful that your hand is attached to your arm? If your hand was attached to your ear, it would cause a lot of problems for your body! We need to be placed properly in the Body of Christ so that we can be effective.

First Corinthians 12:18 tells us that God arranges us just where He wants us to be: *"But in fact God has arranged the parts in the body, every one of them, just as He wanted them to be."* It is important that we know where God has placed us in His Church so that we can serve effectively. You see, it is not the church of *our* choice, but it is the church of *His* choice.

There are different sizes and shapes of churches in our communities in which we can get involved. What I call a "community church" is a traditional church, meeting in a building on a Sunday and reaching the local populace in the surrounding community. It is often about 50-500 in size. A "mega-church" also meets in a church building on a weekend, but it reaches a much broader geographical area. It is often well over 1,000 in size. Finally, what I call a "house church network" is a group of individual house churches, often meeting in homes, which are complete little churches led by their own elders and other spiritual leaders. Each house church (meeting together at least once each week), works with other house churches and other types of churches in their area.

Where is God placing you in the Body of Christ? There are many wonderful churches throughout the world today. The issue is not which church is best. Every church family has strengths and weaknesses. The issue is this: where has God called you to be placed in His Church? Which group of believers has the Lord called you to labor with during this season of your life?

The Lord wants you to grow spiritually, and He wants to use you to reach other people for Christ. Find a church family that you can relate to and then get involved in reaching out to people. Perhaps the Lord wants to use your home as a place where a small group of believers can meet and grow spiritually. Open up your home. You can reproduce yourself spiritually by mentoring or discipling others to grow in their Christian lives. Find your niche in the Body of Christ.

FAMILIES WILL MULTIPLY

We read in the Book of Acts that the early Church grew and multiplied. The Lord had given them His Holy Spirit and a clear strategy from His Word for the Church to grow. These early believers remembered the words of our Lord Jesus before He went back to His Father in Heaven. He told them to *"...go and make disciples of all nations..."* (Matt. 28:19). A few weeks later, as they met from house to house throughout the city of Jerusalem, believers realized that they were responsible to help other new believers grow in their relationship with God.

This is called the principle of multiplication. Believers in small groups are taught and trained to grow in the Lord, and many will eventually be trained to lead their own small groups. This causes the Church to rapidly multiply. The believers in each new group continue to supply what the other believers need in order to grow spiritually, according to Ephesians 4:16.

In order for the local church congregation and small groups in the local church to stay healthy, they need to get a vision from God to grow in numbers and then to multiply to start other groups. The early Church rapidly increased.

In those days when the number of disciples was increasing...the word of God spread. The number of disciples in Jerusalem increased rapidly... (Acts 6:1,7).

The Church of Jesus Christ was multiplied. Every group of believers meeting in a small group needs to have a vision to multiply and start other cell groups or house churches. In this way the Church will continue to be healthy and strong. People in a church or small group that does not reach out to bring people to Christ often stagnate and eventually die spiritually.

Our bodies are made up of cells. Cells in our body go through a process called mitosis. The process of mitosis is simply this: one cell divides and becomes two. Those two cells then in turn divide and become four. In our bodies, a cell that will not produce will eventually die. The same principle applies to the Church of Jesus Christ. Believers in cell groups and house churches are called by God to have a vision to reach out to new people and see them saved and become a part of the Body of Christ. As they grow, people are being multiplied through "spiritual mitosis."

God has called each of us and every local church to pray, to evangelize, and to make disciples. Let's expect the Lord to use us as He multiplies His life through us to others.

ENDNOTE

1. For more on house churches, read Larry Kreider and Floyd McClung, *Starting a House Church* (Ventura, CA: Regal Books, 2007); www .h2hp.com.

SPIRITUAL FAMILY RELATIONSHIPS REFLECTION QUESTIONS

1. Describe the way that your local group of believers is related to other groups. Do you feel like a part of the Church family?

2. Why are new wineskins important to new Christians?

3. What happens when people are built together in relationship?

4. Why does God want us in a particular place in His Church (see 1 Cor. 12:18)?

Chapter 7

WHO IS WATCHING
OUT FOR YOU?

COMMITMENT TO OTHER BELIEVERS

The early Christians had a very effective way of looking out for each other. They met from house to house in small groups so that they could practice loving each other:

> *Practice loving each other, for love comes from God and those who are loving and kind show that they are the children of God, and that they are getting to know Him better* (1 John 4:7 TLB).

Love does not just happen. It must be practiced. It is not just a feeling of goodwill but a decision that motivates us to help people and meet their needs. We cannot practically be committed to love and care for hundreds or thousands of other people. Although we can worship and learn from the Word of God together in a large group, we can only be practically committed to a small group of people at a time. Paul ministered in large public meetings as well as in small house groups, according to Acts 20:20: "...I...have taught you publicly and from house to house."

Practical Christianity happens when believers meet together to reach their neighbors and co-workers with the Gospel of Jesus

Christ and to help each other mature in Christ. Believers in my church family regularly meet in small groups where we pray for those who are sick and hurting as we extend God's love and forgiveness to each other. Our commitment to each other is heartfelt and real. We really do look out for each other. Our small group is our spiritual family.

In some churches, believers show their commitment to other believers in their small group or house church by making a simple pledge to commit to them as their local church family. Making this commitment is not so much a doctrine or a philosophy but a commitment to Jesus and His people to look out for each other. I believe that a commitment to the local church is a commitment to God, His Word, and other believers more than it is a commitment to an institution or an organization. We really show our commitment to other believers in our small group by faithfully interacting and building relationships with them. They will know that we care if we make them a priority in our lives.

Although the elders of our church are the ones who watch out for our spiritual welfare (as we will see in the next section), I am very grateful for the believers in my small group who practically serve me, pray for me, and encourage me in my walk with Jesus Christ.

LEADERS GIVE US SPIRITUAL PROTECTION

According to Hebrews 13:7,17, God places spiritual leaders in our lives who are accountable to God to watch out for us:

Remember your leaders, who spoke the word of God to you. Consider the outcome of their way of life and imitate their faith....Obey your leaders and submit to their authority. They keep watch over you as men who must give an account. Obey them so that their work will be a joy, not a burden, for that would be of no advantage to you.

Spiritual leaders in our lives give us spiritual protection, and we need to follow their example as they place their faith in Jesus Christ. We should remember them, receive the Word of God from them, obey them, be submissive to them, and do all that we can so that their responsibility is joyful and not grievous. The Bible tells us that the devil is like a roaring lion seeking to devour us (see 1 Pet. 5:8). That's why we need church leaders—to protect and encourage us.

According to First Thessalonians 5:12-13, the Lord has called us to recognize and honor those whom He has placed in our lives as spiritual leaders:

Now we ask you, brothers, to respect those who work hard among you, who are over you in the Lord and who admonish you. Hold them in the highest regard in love because of their work. Live in peace with each other.

I have spent much of my time traveling to various nations of the world in the past years, and I have been blessed over and over again by the spiritual leaders that the Lord has placed in my life. Our small group leaders, local pastors, and elders have provided a tremendous sense of encouragement and protection to me and my family. Many times these precious brothers and sisters in Christ have prayed for, encouraged, and exhorted us. These spiritual leaders have encouraged me and held me accountable to take enough time with my family, even though my travel schedule can be hectic. I am grateful to God that my spiritual leaders have my best interests at heart.

LEADERS HELP KEEP US ON TRACK

The Bible tells us in Acts 2:42 that the early believers *"...continued steadfastly in the apostles' doctrine and fellowship, in the breaking of bread, and in prayers"* (NKJV). The early believers continued to study the Scriptures and learn from the preaching and teaching of the early church leaders. Paul the apostle told the Ephesian elders in Acts 20:28-31 that the enemy will try to bring heresy into the Church of Jesus Christ:

> *Keep watch over yourselves and all the flock of which the Holy Spirit has made you overseers. Be shepherds of the church of God, which He bought with His own blood. I know that after I leave, savage wolves will come in among you and will not spare the flock. Even from your own number men will arise and distort the truth in order to draw away disciples after them. So be on your guard! Remember that for three years I never stopped warning each of you night and day with tears.*

The Lord has given us His Word and places spiritual leaders in our lives to keep us from heresy (wrong teaching that is spiritually destructive). There are many "voices" today vying for our attention. We can trust the Word of God, and we can trust spiritual leaders who have good "fruit" (character and integrity) in their lives (see Matt. 7:15-20).

I am grateful for the spiritual leaders whom God has raised up worldwide. There is no one church or family of churches (denomination) that has all of the truth. We need to study the Word of God and learn from spiritual leaders, not only in our local church, but also in the greater Body of Christ. Spiritual leaders help us to keep from becoming sidetracked by minor issues (see Rom. 14:5) and heresies that would try to come into the Body of Christ.

LEADERS EQUIP

God calls believers with spiritual leadership abilities to build up and strengthen the believers in the Church so that all believers can fulfill their work of service. God releases specific leadership gifts in the Body of Christ so that the people with those gifts can equip us for service according to Ephesians 4:11-12:

> *It was He who gave some to be apostles, some to be prophets, some to be evangelists, and some to be pastors and teachers, to prepare God's people for works of service, so that the body of Christ may be built up.*

These five ministry gifts (apostle, prophet, evangelist, pastor, and teacher) are given to various individuals in the Body of Christ who are then responsible to train and equip others. The gifts are "deposited" in spiritual leaders who are called by the Lord to train us to minister to others effectively. Those who have these gifts are able to train each believer for a lifetime of ministry.

Apostles are given to the Church as foundation-layers and as spiritual parents. They have the ability to attract and birth other leaders as they lay the foundations for new churches. Prophets are given to train us to listen to the voice of God. Evangelists are called of God to train us and to "stir us up" to reach the lost. Pastors are commissioned by the Lord to encourage us, protect us, and show us how to make disciples. Teachers have a divine anointing to assist us in understanding the Word of God. Some spiritual leaders may have more than one gift in operation in their lives.

God's plan is to use these five gifts in His local church as much as possible to equip us (the saints) for the work of ministry. When we are equipped, we will be able to minister, too. Every believer is a minister. A pastor or church leader is not the only one who can minister. Every believer is called to minister to others in Jesus' name. You can receive input from someone with a spiritual leadership ability (gift) and be equipped and strengthened as you come to maturity as a Christian.

LEADERS LEAD

What can we learn from the New Testament about how leadership works practically in a local church? Acts 15 tells about a dispute in the Church and how they solved it. Paul, sent out as an apostle, met with the leadership of the church in Jerusalem to discuss a problem. James was the clear leader of the Jerusalem church along with a team of elders who worked with him: *"The next day Paul and the rest of us went to see James, and all the elders were present"* (Acts 21:18).

James and his team of elders were responsible to work out solutions to problems as they prayed and heard from the Father. At every local church, there should be a team of elders, along with one person who is called to give clear oversight to this team and the local church. In fact, this principle applies in every area of the church. God calls teams of people to work together for a common goal; however, someone always has been chosen by the Lord to be the leader of this team: *"May the Lord, the God of the spirits of all mankind, appoint a man over this community"* (Num. 27:16).

Every local church, every family of churches, and every cell group or house church needs to have a clear leadership team, along with someone who has been chosen of God to give leadership to the team.[1] For example, in a husband-wife relationship, there is a real sense of teamwork. In a healthy marriage, the husband and wife make decisions together; however, the husband is called to be the head of the home and should love and care for his wife. When, in times of crisis, a decision has to be made, the husband is responsible for the final decision.

When an airplane is flying, everyone works together as a team. However, during times of crisis, take off, and landing, who is in charge? The pilot. This is based on a spiritual truth. For instance, in your local church, God has called someone to give clear leadership to the church, yet at the same time, there should be a real sense of teamwork among the leadership team.

Acts 14:21-23 tells us that Paul and Barnabas were concerned that every local church in every area had clear eldership (spiritual leadership) appointed among them. In the New Testament, we see various types of spiritual leadership mentioned. Acts 15:6 says, *"The apostles and elders met to consider this question."* The elders were those who gave oversight to the local congregations. The apostles were those who had a larger sphere of oversight because they were called to oversee church leaders from various parts of the world. As "apostolic overseers," they were responsible to care for, oversee, encourage, and equip local elders who served the people in their local area or sphere of influence: *"We, however, will not boast beyond measure, but within the limits of the sphere which God appointed us—a sphere which especially includes you"* (2 Cor. 10:13 NKJV).

Paul the apostle told the Corinthian believers that they were within his sphere of responsibility. Paul was not a local elder in the Corinthian church; however, he was responsible to give oversight to the eldership who oversaw the work of God in that area. Paul called himself an apostle. Various denominations use different terminology when referring to these apostolic overseers in today's church; however, they still fulfill a similar role of overseeing pastors and elders in the local church.

CHOSEN BY GOD, CONFIRMED BY PEOPLE

Since it is the Lord's plan for His Church to grow and multiply, He constantly desires to release new leaders in His Church. The leadership at the church of Antioch came together to fast and pray, and then the Holy Spirit called Barnabas and Saul to a new work of planting churches:

> *In the church at Antioch there were prophets and teachers...While they were worshiping the Lord and fasting, the Holy Spirit said, "Set apart for me Barnabas and Saul for the work to which I have called them." So after they had fasted and prayed, they placed their hands on them and sent them off* (Acts 13:1-4).

Barnabas and Saul were sent out to do God's work by the Holy Spirit. The Holy Spirit is the One who calls church leaders and believers into areas of ministry. After they were called, the spiritual leaders at Antioch affirmed the new leaders, laid their hands on them, and prayed for them to be sent away to fulfill the Lord's call on their lives.

In today's church, different church families have various ways of choosing leadership. Some churches are governed by a democracy. A democracy is basically a church ruled by the people. Either a committee is formed or there is a type of consensus or vote to make decisions about church leadership.

Others are governed by a theocracy. I am of the persuasion that God is restoring theocracy to His Church. Church government by theocracy means the leadership of the church fast and pray, and the Holy Spirit speaks to them about whom He is calling to spiritual leadership. God's people then, through fasting and prayer, give their affirmation to the Holy Spirit calling this person to spiritual leadership. In the New Testament, spiritual leaders were called by God in this way.

It is my understanding that leadership in a local church (or in a cell group) should be appointed because *God* is the One who has called this spiritual leader into an area of oversight and spiritual service. When God calls a person to leadership, he or she will be confirmed by other leaders and the Body of Christ. Remember David the shepherd boy who was called to be the king of Israel? The Lord called David as a young boy. He was anointed with oil through Samuel the prophet (see 1 Sam. 16:13); however, it was not until many years later that David was affirmed by others to be the new king of Israel. Between the time of his call and the time of the fulfillment of this prophecy, David experienced many dark hours hiding out from a demonized king who was trying to kill him. But the day came when David was confirmed to be the king of Israel by other leaders around him and then eventually by the people of God.

I believe that it is also advantageous to have spiritual leaders from outside the local congregation involved in this process of discernment regarding leadership. In Titus 1:5, Paul tells Titus to be responsible for the process of choosing leadership in the churches in

Crete: *"The reason I left you in Crete was that you might straighten out what was left unfinished and appoint elders in every town, as I directed you."* Anyone who has been given authority by the Lord needs to also be under authority. Titus was serving under Paul's leadership as an apostle in the early Church.

LEADERS ARE ALWAYS SERVANTS

Leaders in the Body of Christ are called to be servants. Jesus Christ was the greatest leader who ever lived, and He said,

> *...whoever wants to become great among you must be your servant, and whoever wants to be first must be your slave— just as the Son of Man did not come to be served, but to serve, and to give His life as a ransom for many* (Matthew 20:26b-28).

If someone comes to me and says that he feels called to be a leader, I am not impressed with how much charisma he has or with his knowledge of the Bible. The real key to his ability to lead depends on whether or not he loves Jesus, loves His people, and is willing to serve.

Churches often acknowledge individuals within their congregation who have a special ministry in serving as "deacons." The Bible tells us that deacons were first to be tested before they were set apart as deacons (see 1 Tim. 3:10). When someone desires to be involved in any type of church leadership, there should first be a period of time for him to be tested. Does he really have the heart of a servant? This is not implying that there is something wrong with him; it simply means that he needs to have time to see how he fits in with the other believers in the local church.

People are like pieces to a puzzle. Some people fit together, and others do not. That's the way it is in the Kingdom of God. It takes time until we know whether or not God has placed people together so that they can work smoothly and effectively with one another.

Sometimes problems in churches occur because the pastor or leader was brought in with good intentions, but the pieces just didn't seem to fit. If my arm is broken, a doctor would set it with a cast. It would take some time for it to be bonded back together. People need time to be bonded together. As the Lord calls you to be involved in a local church, allow the Lord to take enough time for you to be knit together in relationships with those in the church. It takes time for these relationships to be built. Relationships are built on trust, and trust takes time. These relationships can be built effectively with a small group of believers.

Consequently, when someone comes into a local church and becomes a part of a small group, wise spiritual leaders will give God the time He needs to work in the life of this believer before placing him into spiritual leadership. As the grace of God is evident in the believer's life, it will not be long until people around him will begin to look to him for leadership. Spiritual leaders who are sensitive to the Holy Spirit will begin to release him into areas of leadership, perhaps as an assistant leader in the small group. This can be a training ground for future leadership.

ENDNOTE

1. For more about elders in the Church, read Larry Kreider, Ron Myer, Steve Prokopchak, and Brian Sauder, *The Biblical Role of Elders in the Church* by (Lititz, PA: House to House Publications, 2003); www.h2hp.com.

WHO IS WATCHING OUT FOR YOU?
REFLECTION QUESTIONS

1. How is a small home group a great way to promote true fellowship? How have you helped to meet the needs of others in your small group?

2. List ways that your spiritual leaders have watched out for you.

3. Have you been equipped and released in a particular gift so that you can minister to others?

4. Why is it important to have clear leadership for a team?

Chapter 8

OUR COMMITMENT TO THE LOCAL CHURCH

COMMON VISION

Did you ever go to a church meeting and feel like it was a really nice group of believers, but somehow you just didn't fit in? Although there was nothing wrong with this church, God simply wasn't calling you there. Every believer needs to be placed within the Body of Christ so that he or she will be working hand-in-hand with believers who share a common vision. At the same time, we need to confirm the rest of the Body of Christ around us so that God's purposes can be fulfilled. Remember, God is a creative God. In the same way that the Lord created you and me, He created various kinds of congregations in His church family. Together they fulfill the purposes of God.

The Scripture says that we should not plow with a donkey and an ox together (see Deut. 22:10). Why? Because they move at different paces. We need to be sure that the people we are "walking with" in our local church are those with whom the Lord has placed us so that we can walk in unity and He can command a blessing.

How good and pleasant it is when brothers live together in unity!...For there the Lord bestows His blessing, even life forevermore (Psalm 133:1,3b).

You can make hamburgers at McDonald's, but if you go to work at another restaurant, they will make hamburgers a bit differently from the way you were trained to do it. Every church has a different way of doing things. They have different visions that the Lord has given them to fulfill.

For example, some churches prefer singing hymns with an organ while others prefer choruses and worship with a band. Some churches may focus more on systematic Bible teaching, while others focus more on evangelism. We need to be a part of a church where we can agree with the basic "values" that the spiritual leaders are teaching us.

In a cell-based church or house church, everyone is a part of a small group where they can be accountable to their brothers and sisters in the way that they live their Christian lives. These smaller groups have a vision to nurture believers and help them with "blind spots" in their lives.

A church's vision encourages us to support and submit to the leadership that God raises up among us. When a church body agrees to a common vision, it will be easier to "live together in unity!"

KNOW WHERE YOU ARE CALLED

Maybe you are saying, "How do I really know where God has placed me in His Church?" First of all, you need to pray. Ask God, "Who are the Christian believers with whom I have a relationship?" Remember, the Lord places His people in relationships so that they can serve Him. The Scripture also tells us that we must *"...let the peace of Christ rule in our hearts"* (Col. 3:15). In other words, you will know where you fit as you pray and take steps of faith and obedience.

We are living in the last days, and God tells us that He is going to pour out His Spirit on all flesh. You can expect it to happen. The Bible says in Acts 2:17-18:

> *"In the last days," God says, "I will pour out My Spirit on all people. Your sons and daughters will prophesy, your young men will see visions, your old men will dream dreams. Even on My servants, both men and women, I will pour out My Spirit in those days, and they will prophesy."*

When the Lord poured out His Spirit in Acts, chapter 2, the Church was birthed in Jerusalem. Believers met from house to house all over the city. As God pours out His Spirit in our generation, there will be a need for many new "wineskins." New churches will be raised up to take care of the coming harvest as new believers are birthed into the Kingdom of God. Some may be community churches, others mega-churches, and still others house churches. God may call you to be part of a new fellowship of believers in the future.

Trust God to lead you to spiritual leaders who are open and transparent with their own lives. Spiritual leaders need to be transparent with their Christian lives, sharing their weaknesses as well as their strengths.

Ask the Lord to lead you to believers who will be willing to pray with you to help you discern where the Lord is placing you in His Body. God wants you connected to a local church where you can be trained, protected, and available to serve others.

AGREEMENT IN THE LOCAL CHURCH

All believers in a local church should know what their church believes. Every local church should also have a clear "statement of faith" and a written statement of the specific vision that the Lord has given them to fulfill. Billy Graham and a group of spiritual leaders met in Lausanne, Switzerland, in 1974, and the Lord gave them a statement of faith called the *Lausanne Covenant*. This is the covenant that our church, along with thousands of other churches throughout the world, has used as a statement of faith. This statement of faith declares that there is one God and that the Bible is the inspired Word of God. It states all of the major doctrines that are so precious to us as true believers in Jesus Christ.[1] If you are considering joining a church family, ask for their statement of faith.

Beyond your knowledge of and agreement with your church's statement of faith, God wants you to be involved in a church where the church leadership and all of God's people work together in unity: *"Make every effort to keep the unity of the Spirit through the bond of peace"* (Eph. 4:3).

As we preserve the unity in our local church family, God will continue to pour out His blessing on us. If someone comes to you regarding a problem with leadership in your local church, tell him that he needs to talk to the person with whom he has the problem. There is no place for gossip or slander in the Kingdom of God. The enemy will use it as a wedge of disunity. If believers in your small group do not agree with the leadership of the local church, they need to pray and then discuss their problem with the leadership, not with other believers in the church. Those in leadership should be open to listening to the concerns of those they lead. Godly leaders will want to hear your appeals. The enemy knows that a breakdown of unity will hinder the work of God more than any other thing in the local church. That's why the Scripture says in First Corinthians 1:10 that we should appeal to each other:

> *I appeal to you, brothers, in the name of our Lord Jesus Christ, that all of you agree with one another so that there may be no divisions among you and that you may be perfectly united in mind and thought.*

SUPPORT YOUR CHURCH'S VISION

If every person called to be a part of a local church is committed to a relationship with a small group of believers within the church, there will be healthy relationships throughout the church. In the New Testament, God's people met as small groups of believers in homes. Everyone was needed:

> *Now the body is not made up of one part but of many. If the foot should say, "Because I am not a hand, I do not belong to the body," it would not for that reason cease to be part of the body. And if the ear should say, "Because I am not an eye, I do not belong to the body," it would not for that reason cease to be part of the body. If the whole body were an eye, where would the sense of hearing be? If the whole body were an ear, where would the sense of smell be? But in fact God has arranged the parts in the body, every one of them, just as He wanted them to be* (1 Corinthians 12:14-18).

Just as every member of the human body is important, every member of the local church should know where and how he or she is connected to the Body of our Lord Jesus Christ. If you have questions about the specific vision of your church, it is important that you sit down with church leadership to gain a clear understanding of what the Lord has called your church to do.

It is of utmost importance that believers support the vision and the leadership of the local church in which they serve. If you cannot support the leadership and the vision of your church, then the Lord may be calling you into another local church.

Did you ever notice how a group of houses in a community may all look the same on the outside because they were built by a builder with one particular style? Most of these houses, however, are different inside. In the same way, although they may "look" similar, various churches have different callings from the Lord and, as a spiritual family, have their own uniqueness. God has called us to be committed to Him, His Word, and His people in a practical way through the local church.

UNIFIED BUT NOT EXCLUSIVE

It is important to have the same basic vision within a church family because, if we do not dwell together in unity, God cannot command a blessing (see Ps. 133:1-3). But we cannot be exclusive. In the Book of First Corinthians, one of the believers said, "I am of Paul," and another said, "I am of Apollos;" another said, "I am of Cephas (or Peter)," and another said, "I am of Christ" (see 1 Cor. 1:12).

Paul wrote back and told them that this was wrong. "Is Christ divided?" he asked. There can be no division in the Body of Christ, neither should it be exclusive. The Lord warns us of considering one church (or one small group or house church) as better than another.

The Scripture says in First Corinthians 12:5-6, *"There are different kinds of service, but the same Lord. There are different kinds of working, but the same God works all of them in all men."*

We are called to love and encourage people from many different churches. However, we also need to be committed to and in unity with those in our church family, whether in our small group, local congregation, or house church.

Sometimes believers want to change from one local church to another. If someone believes the Lord is asking him to become involved in another church, he should talk to his trusted spiritual leaders first. If there is a difficulty in his former church, he needs to go the "hundredth" mile to be sure he has a clear relationship with that church and their leadership. If he doesn't, his problem may follow him.

When our church began in 1980, we were commissioned out of our former church. Although our new church has a different "personality" than the church we were commissioned from, we still have a wonderful relationship with the precious people in our former church.

A UNIFIED CHURCH WILL MULTIPLY

One kernel of corn planted in a field will produce approximately 1,200 kernels of corn. If these 1,200 kernels of corn are planted the following year, they will produce 1,440,000 kernels of corn. This is called the principle of multiplication. Every church should multiply. One person shares with another person the good news of Jesus. This person receives Christ into his life and shares with another. And the church grows. Growing churches start new churches!

The Lord's desire is for His Church to go forth in power and authority as Christians go from house to house in every community, throughout every city, town, and nation of the world. In a vision that the Lord gave me many years ago, I saw missiles shooting out of our home area to the nations of the world. These missiles represented believers who were sent out to other nations to share the Gospel of Jesus Christ and to plant new churches. God wants to use you in your local church to touch the world.

Every church needs a local, national, and international vision. Churches without a mission vision will eventually stagnate. Jesus says in Matthew 28:19-20 that we should go and make disciples of all nations. That's why He left us on this planet. Years ago, our local church had the privilege of encouraging a new church to start in Nairobi, Kenya. Today more than 75 churches in Kenya, Uganda, and Rwanda have grown out of that initial church plant with a vision to reach into the nations of Africa and beyond.

God wants Christians to work together, stand together, and pray together as He builds His Church through small groups of believers. In small groups, Christians can be trained and then sent out as a spiritual army to take localities and the nations of the world back from the devil. Jesus Christ will continue to add to His Church. The Bible says that the early Church was *"praising God and enjoying the favor of all the people. And the Lord added to their number daily those who were being saved"* (Acts 2:47).

Although God's purpose for us in our churches, small groups, and house churches is to reach people for Christ, we will experience fellowship with one another at the same time. Fellowship with others is an added blessing to those who are serving Jesus. However, may we never forget why the Lord has placed us on this earth—*to know Him and to make Him known.*

UNDERSTAND YOUR CHURCH'S ROOTS

Throughout the Bible, we see examples of the Lord asking His people to set up monuments and altars as a remembrance of the things that the Lord had done. In First Samuel 7, the prophet set up a stone as a reminder to God's people that the Lord had helped them. The Bible tells us in Deuteronomy 4:9:

> *Only be careful, and watch yourselves closely so that you do not forget the things your eyes have seen or let them slip from your heart as long as you live. Teach them to your children and to their children after them.*

God was concerned that the children of Israel would forget the phenomenal things that He had done throughout their history. He commanded them to teach their children and grandchildren.

When you join a church family, it is important to understand its "roots." Find out why God "birthed" your church. Understanding the past will give you a clear sense of what makes your local church tick. You will see the faithfulness of God.

Ask your pastors or elders for a book or articles that were written about the early days of your church family or denomination. The history of our church family is printed in a book.[1] We encourage everyone who is called to be a part of our church family to read this book so that he or she can understand where we've come from and what the Lord has called us to do.

Someone once said, "We build on the shoulders of those who have gone on before us." Many times mistakes are made because we have not heeded the lessons learned by our spiritual forefathers.

Although each local church needs to have a clear vision, we must remember that nothing happens except by the grace of God. The responsibility to make something happen is God's. You and I simply need to be obedient. We "plant our seeds" in faith and expect them to grow, but it is not our responsibility to make them grow. We co-labor with God for His glory.

God bless you as you allow the Lord to place you in His Body in a way that pleases Him. Remember, it is not the church of *your* choice, but the church of *His* choice. Expect the Lord to use you as He builds His Church through you from house to house, city to city, and nation to nation.

ENDNOTES

1. A copy of the Lausanne Covenant appears at www.dcfi.org/about.htm.

2. Larry Kreider, *House to House* (Lititz, PA: House to House Publications, 1998); www.h2hp.com.

OUR COMMITMENT TO THE LOCAL CHURCH
REFLECTION QUESTIONS

1. How does your personal vision compare with your church's (or small group's) vision?

2. According to Colossians 3:15, what is the basic evidence that you are where God wants you to be? What should you do if you feel you do not fit in?

3. What is your responsibility in keeping unity in your small group, your church, your family?

4. Research the history of your church family and see how faithful God has been.

PART III

Authority and Accountability

Chapter 9

UNDERSTANDING THE FEAR OF THE LORD AND AUTHORITY

FEAR OF THE LORD CAUSES OBEDIENCE

Jonah was a prophet in the Old Testament who made a major mistake. The Lord called him to go to the wicked city of Nineveh and warn the people of God's impending judgment. But Jonah knew that his God was a compassionate God. He figured that the people in Ninevah would repent and be spared God's judgment, and he really did not want God to have mercy on any nation but Israel. So, instead of obeying, he boarded a ship that was going in the opposite direction to the farthest place possible.

In the midst of the voyage, the Lord sent a huge storm that nearly wiped out the ship. The sailors were frightened as they cried out to their heathen gods. In the turmoil, someone found Jonah asleep in the lower part of the ship. The captain implored Jonah, "What are you doing sleeping? Get up and call on your God; maybe He'll keep us from perishing!"

Even though the sailors did not believe in the true God, they were spiritual men and believed in the supernatural. They cast lots to see whether or not someone on board was the cause of the storm that was about to destroy them. The lot fell on Jonah. Jonah then confessed, *"...I fear the Lord, the God of heaven, who made the sea and the dry land"* (Jon. 1:9 NKJV).

Jonah felt guilty for disobeying God and putting the sailors at risk. He instructed the sailors to pick him up and throw him into the sea and promised that the sea would then stop raging. After repeated attempts to bring the ship to land failed, they reluctantly threw Jonah overboard. Immediately the sea grew calm. *"At this the men greatly feared the Lord, and they offered a sacrifice to the Lord and made vows to Him"* (Jon. 1:16).

These men understood the fear of the Lord. The fear of the Lord causes people to place their faith in the Lord for salvation. It also causes them to realize that God judges sin because He is a holy God. We need to have a healthy understanding of the fear of the Lord because, if we understand it, we will want to live a life of obedience to Him.

FEAR OF THE LORD CAUSES REVERENCE

The Bible tells us in Proverbs 9:10a that, if we have a deep reverence and love for God, we will gain wisdom: *"The fear of the Lord is the beginning of wisdom...."*

A healthy understanding of the fear of the Lord is simply to be awestruck by His power and presence. To fear the Lord is to be in awe of Him and to reverence Him, understanding that we serve a mighty God. Our Father in Heaven loves us perfectly. He wants the best for our lives. He is a God who has created the entire universe and has all power and authority in His hand. As Christians, we should possess a holy fear that trembles at God's Word:

"Has not my hand made all these things, and so they came into being?" declares the Lord. "This is the one I esteem: he

who is humble and contrite in spirit, and trembles at my word" (Isaiah 66:2).

This is not to say that God wants us to cower in a corner. That's not what the fear of the Lord is about. The Lord does not desire for His children to be afraid of Him, but to honor and respect Him. God's Word tells us that *"perfect love casts out fear"* (1 John 4:18 NKJV). In other words, where God's perfect love is, fear cannot dwell; or to say it another way—where there is the presence of fear, there is the absence of love.

However, if we love, honor, and respect our God, we will want to obey Him because the fear of the Lord also involves a fear of sinning against Him and facing the consequences. I grew up with an earthly father who loved me. I was not afraid of him. However, whenever I was disobedient, I feared the consequences of the discipline that I knew would follow. Yet, I knew that even the discipline was from a father who loved me. Our heavenly Father loves us so much, yet He hates sin.

Our God is a God of complete authority in this universe. Ask the Lord to give you the grace to experience the fear of the Lord in your life. Expect to be awestruck by His presence in your life!

FEAR OF THE LORD CAUSES REPENTANCE

When we have a healthy fear of the Lord, we will not want to sin against Him: *"To fear the Lord is to hate evil..."* (Prov. 8:13). We know that sinning against a holy God means that we will have to face the consequences. Although we realize that God is not a God with a big stick just waiting for us to make a mistake, God *will* punish sin.

The Bible tells us in Acts 9:31 that the New Testament Church understood what it meant to walk in the fear of the Lord. When we have a proper understanding of the fear of the Lord, we will hate evil, knowing that evil displeases the Lord and destroys God's people:

> *Do you not know that the wicked will not inherit the kingdom of God? Do not be deceived: Neither the sexually immoral nor idolaters nor adulterers nor male prostitutes nor homosexual offenders nor thieves nor the greedy nor drunkards nor slanderers nor swindlers will inherit the kingdom of God. And that is what some of you were. But you were washed, you were sanctified, you were justified in the name of the Lord Jesus Christ and by the Spirit of our God* (1 Corinthians 6:9-11).

In other words, true Christians will not live a life of sin. The good news is this: when we repent and turn from our sin, Jesus washes us clean. And the fear of the Lord keeps us from going back to our old way of living.

There are many examples of the fear of the Lord in the New Testament. After Ananias and Sapphira lied to the Holy Spirit and were struck dead, God's judgment on their sin caused the believers to increase in their awe and fear of the Lord: *"Great fear seized the whole church and all who heard about these events"* (Acts 5:11).

In Revelation 1:17, John had an encounter with God: *"When I saw Him, I fell at his feet as though dead. Then He placed His right hand on me and said: "Do not be afraid. I am the First and the Last."*

Our fear of the Lord is not a destructive fear but one that leads us to God's presence and purity. When we understand and experience the fear of the Lord, we will hate sin and turn away from it. We will trust Jesus to wash us, cleanse us, and make us new.

WHY AUTHORITY?

The Lord has chosen to give His authority to men and women in various areas, including the government, our employment, the Church, and our families. If we understand the fear of the Lord in a healthy way, we will understand why God places authorities in our lives. The Lord delegates responsibility to the authorities so that He can use them to mold us, adjust us, and structure our lives. If we resist these authorities, Scripture indicates that we are resisting God and bringing judgment upon ourselves. Romans 13:1-4a tells us:

> *Everyone must submit himself to the governing authorities, for there is no authority except that which God has established. The authorities that exist have been established by God. Consequently, he who rebels against the authority is rebelling against what God has instituted, and those who do so will bring judgment on themselves. For rulers hold no terror for those who do right, but for those who do wrong. Do you want to be free from fear of the one in authority? Then do what is right and he will commend you. For he is God's servant to do you good....*

The authorities that are in our lives have been placed there by God. For example, police officers and government officials are ministers of God. That does not mean that they are being obedient to God all of the time. However, God has placed them in our lives and wants us to respond to them in a godly way. If we're driving through a town and a police officer stands at an intersection and puts up his hand, every driver will stop because of his authority. It is not his own authority, but the authority of the government that he represents. If we disobey the police officer, we are disobeying the government because the police officer is under authority.

A proper understanding of authority will bring security into our lives. The Scriptures teach us that *"rulers hold no terror for those who do right, but for those who do wrong"* (Rom. 13:3). When there is no authority, there is chaos. One of the darkest periods of history for the people of God occurred because no authority was set in place: *"In those days Israel had no king; everyone did as he saw fit"* (Judg. 21:25). Society does not tolerate chaos. There is always a need for some form of government or type of authority structure. If we do not have a godly authority structure, the vacuum will cause an ungodly authority structure to develop.

God delegates His authority to men and women. Anyone who has authority needs to be under authority, or he becomes a tyrant. I once heard a story of a sergeant in the army who relished his authority, taking great pleasure in telling men to obey his orders. When he retired, he attempted to apply the same principles in his hometown. He would bark an order at a store clerk, or a mail carrier, or a waiter in a restaurant. Needless to say, he was not very well received! The ex-sergeant soon realized that he no longer had authority over those people because he was no longer under (military) authority.

If we are not under the authority of Jesus, we can attempt to resist the devil and the demons of hell, but they do not need to submit to us. However, when we are submitted to God's authority in our lives, the devil must flee.

SUBMITTING TO AUTHORITY

The Lord has set up delegated authorities to protect us and to help us be conformed to the image of Christ. For many people, this is a hard lesson to learn. There was a young man who was not willing to submit to the authority of his parents, so he decided to join the army. Guess what? Then he *really* learned what submitting to authority was all about!

What does it mean to "submit to authority?" The word *submit* means "to yield oneself to the authority or will of another; to defer to or consent to abide by the opinion or authority of another."[1] Submission is an attitude of the heart that desires to obey God and the human authorities that He has placed in our lives.

The word *authority* means a "power to influence or command."[2] In other words, it is the right given by God to men and women to build, mold, adjust, and structure the lives of others. An authority is a person who has been given responsibility for our lives. At our workplace, it's our employer; in our hometown, it is our local government official; in the Body of Christ, our authorities are the elders and pastors of our church; and for young people who are living at home, it is their parents.

Paul reminds believers in Titus 3:1 that it is important to be obedient to the authorities in their lives: *"Remind the people to be subject to rulers and authorities, to be obedient, to be ready to do whatever is good."*

Submission to authority is not a popular topic today. Employees rebel against their employers, school children against their teachers, children against their parents, and churchgoers against their pastors. The Lord wants to restore a proper understanding of the fear of the Lord and submission to authority to our generation. If we do not learn to properly submit to the authorities that the Lord has placed in our lives, we are disobedient to God who has placed these authorities there.

Submission to authority seems foolish to many people, but *"...God chose the foolish things of the world to shame the wise; God chose the weak things of the world to shame the strong"* (1 Cor. 1:27).

Whenever I resist any authority that the Lord has placed in my life—parents, employer, police, church authority—I am actually resisting God. (Unless, of course, the authority is asking me to do something that violates God's Word and causes me to sin.) I have told young people, "When your parents ask you to be in by midnight or an employer tells you to be at work on time, the Lord is using these authorities to train and mold you into the character of Christ. If you don't obey, you will have to learn the same hard lessons over and over again."

OBEDIENCE IS BETTER THAN "SACRIFICE"

God always requires obedience to His Word. In First Samuel 15:22-23, Saul rebelled and disobeyed God's clear instructions because he placed his own perception of what was right above what God said. Saul had been commanded to wait until the prophet Samuel came to offer a sacrifice. However, Saul feared the people instead of fearing God, and he went ahead and offered the sacrifice. Samuel's admonition was very direct and to the point:

...Does the Lord delight in burnt offerings and sacrifices as much as in obeying the voice of the Lord? To obey is better than sacrifice, and to heed is better than the fat of rams. For rebellion is like the sin of divination, and arrogance like the evil of idolatry....

Obeying from the heart is better than "sacrifice" (any outward form of service for the Lord). Rebellion (disobedience) is equated with the sin of witchcraft. Later, the Bible tells us that an evil spirit tormented Saul (see 1 Sam. 16:14). Saul's rebellion allowed room for an evil spirit to come into his life, and he lived as a tormented man for the rest of his life. He had refused to walk in the fear of the Lord.

Unless we learn to submit to the authorities that the Lord has placed in our lives, we cannot respond appropriately as an authority to others. Children who do not obey their parents and do not repent for their disobedience grow up with an unwholesome understanding of authority. They are often domineering over their own children. If we have not properly responded to the authorities that the Lord has placed in our lives, the Lord may require us to ask forgiveness of the person(s) we have dishonored. Our confession can break the bondage of rebellion and stubbornness that may be operating in our lives.

DELEGATED AUTHORITY MOLDS US

The authorities that the Lord has placed in our lives will not be perfect. We do not submit to them because they are perfect, but we submit to them because the Lord has placed them there. I remember one of the jobs that I had as a young man. I did not like the attitude of my employer. But, regardless of his attitude, I submitted to him because he was my employer. I have learned that it is a tremendous blessing to obey the authorities that the Lord has placed in my life.

Wherever we go, one of the first questions that we should ask ourselves is, "Who has the Lord placed in authority here?" People who are truly under God's authority see authority everywhere they go. They realize that these authorities have been delegated and appointed by the Lord. Luke 17:7-10 explains this delegated authority:

> *Suppose one of you had a servant plowing or looking after the sheep. Would he say to the servant when he comes in from*

the field, "Come along now and sit down to eat"? Would he not rather say, "Prepare my supper, get yourself ready and wait on me while I eat and drink; after that you may eat and drink"? Would he thank the servant because he did what he was told to do? So you also, when you have done everything you were told to do, should say, "We are unworthy servants; we have only done our duty"

This slave, after working hard all day, came in from the field and prepared his master's meal first. Did his master thank him? No, because it was the *responsibility* of the servant to prepare the food for his master. The servant had a clear understanding of God's delegated authority. Secure people have no problem with submitting to the authorities that the Lord has placed in their lives.

It is our responsibility to submit to the authorities that the Lord has placed in our lives, in our homes, employment, community, and in the Church. The Lord works His character in us as we learn this important principle. I have seen it happen over and over again when someone cannot submit to his employer—in most cases, he goes from job to job with the same problem because the problem lies with the employee. The Lord uses His delegated authorities to teach us, mold us, and build the character of Christ in our lives. We, then, can be His loving authorities to others whom He places in our lives.

ENDNOTES

1. *Merriam-Webster's Collegiate Dictionary*, 11th ed., s.v. "Submit."
2. *Merriam-Webster's Collegiate Dictionary*, 11th ed., s.v. "Authority."

UNDERSTANDING THE FEAR OF THE LORD AND AUTHORITY
REFLECTION QUESTIONS

1. If God does not want us to be afraid of Him, what kind of "fear" are we talking about?

2. Who are the governing authorities in your life? List ways that each one is used by the Lord to mold, adjust, and structure your life.

3. What does authority mean? How is resisting authority in your life actually resisting God?

4. Explain the phrase "obedience is better than sacrifice" (see 1 Sam. 15:22-23).

Chapter 10

DELEGATED AUTHORITY IN GOVERNMENT, WORKPLACE, FAMILY, AND CHURCH

HONORING AUTHORITY IN GOVERNMENT

In this chapter, we're going to look at four basic areas where God has delegated His authority to men and women. These four areas include the government, the workplace, the family, and the church.

First of all, let's look at government. In the fallen world we live in, we need order and restraints to protect us from chaos. That's why God ordained government. According to Romans 13:1-2, we are to submit to the governing authorities:

> *Everyone must submit himself to the governing authorities, for there is no authority except that which God has established...Consequently, he who rebels against the authority is rebelling against what God has instituted....*

Christians should obey the governing authorities because they are instituted by God. Romans 13:5-7 says that we should be subject to authorities not because we are afraid of punishment but because they have been ordained by God; we keep a clear conscience by obeying them:

> *Therefore, it is necessary to submit to the authorities, not only because of possible punishment but also because of conscience. This is also why you pay taxes, for the authorities are God's servants, who give their full time to governing. Give everyone what you owe him: If you owe taxes, pay taxes; if revenue, then revenue; if respect, then respect; if honor, then honor.*

This Scripture says that, if we complain about paying taxes, we are complaining about the authorities that the Lord has placed in our lives. Sometimes we tend to speak negatively about authorities—police officers, for example. We especially do this when they give us a ticket for a traffic violation! We must remember that police officers are God's ministers. We need to relate to them with a submissive attitude of honor.

Daniel, in the Old Testament, was taken to Babylon as a slave when he was 16 years old. Even so, he lived in the fear of the Lord and was a man of prayer. He learned to honor the leadership in Babylon and was appointed prime minister under three different administrations.

Whether or not authorities in our lives are godly or ungodly people, the Lord has placed them there. One time, the apostle Paul was taken before the religious council. The high priest, Ananias, commanded those who stood by Paul to strike him on the mouth. Paul didn't realize Ananias was the high priest and responded by calling him a *"whitewashed wall"* (Acts 23:3). Those standing by said, "How can you insult God's high priest?" Paul immediately apologized, *"...Brothers, I did not realize that he was the high priest; for it is written: 'Do not speak evil about the ruler of your people'"* (Acts 23:5).

Even though the authorities in our lives may be ungodly, the Lord has called us to have an attitude of submission to them. We honor them for their position, not for their conduct.

HONORING AUTHORITY IN THE WORKPLACE

The second group of authorities that the Lord has placed in our lives is our employers. Paul urges Christians to regard their jobs as service to the Lord:

> *Slaves, [employees] obey your earthly masters* [employers] *in everything; and do it, not only when their eye is on you and to win their favor, but with sincerity of heart and reverence for the Lord. Whatever you do, work at it with all your heart, as working for the Lord, not for men, since you know that you will receive an inheritance from the Lord as a reward. It is the Lord Christ you are serving* (Colossians 3:22-24).

In other words, our real employer is Jesus Christ. We need to see our jobs as service to the Lord Jesus Christ. If we have a tendency to do our best only when the boss is around, then there's a problem.

I have a friend who worked in a steak restaurant. He submitted to his boss as the authority that he knew the Lord had placed over him. The owners and managers were so impressed with his attitude that they continued to hire his Christian friends. Within a short period of time, the majority of the employees at the restaurant were Christians. Why? Because this young man had an attitude of submission to the authority of his managers and employers.

The Lord has called us to work at our jobs enthusiastically with all of our hearts, realizing that we are doing it unto the Lord. And imagine, as we're doing it unto the Lord, we are getting paid to serve Him in our places of employment!

HOW GOD USES EMPLOYERS

If your boss is a Christian, do not think that he should give you extra favors because you are a believer. Some Christians think, "My boss should understand why I'm late to work or why I'm slow. He is a Christian." Even if he is a believer, your boss needs to take the authority given to him by God and discipline you so that you can be truly conformed into the image of Christ.

All who are under the yoke of slavery [employees] *should consider their masters* [employers] *worthy of full respect, so that God's name and our teaching may not be slandered. Those who have believing masters are not to show less respect for them because they are brothers. Instead, they are to serve them even better, because those who benefit from their service are believers, and dear to them...* (1 Timothy 6:1-2).

Slaves [employees], *submit yourselves to your masters* [employers] *with all respect, not only to those who are good and considerate, but also to those who are harsh. For it is commendable if a man bears up under the pain of unjust suffering because he is conscious of God. But how is it to your credit if you receive a beating for doing wrong and endure it? But if you suffer for doing good and you endure it, this is commendable before God. To this you were called, because Christ suffered for you, leaving you an example, that you should follow in his steps* (1 Peter 2:18-21).

If we are late for work or lazy on the job, our employer needs to deal with us properly so that we can learn to be disciplined men and women of God. However, if we are doing a good job and our employer is harsh or critical, then the Lord promises us that He will reward us.

Jesus and Moses both learned to submit to their employer's authority before the Lord used them effectively. Jesus worked in the carpenter's shop for many years before being thrust into His ministry (see Mark 6:3). Moses was herding sheep for his father-in-law for 40 years as God prepared him to lead the Lord's people out of the bondage of Egypt (see Exod. 3:1). Their heavenly Father used these authorities in their lives to teach them to have a submissive spirit toward Him and a spirit of patience toward the people whom they served.

HONORING AUTHORITY IN THE FAMILY

The Lord has instructed us to submit to the authorities that He has placed in our lives. Families are another area of submission. Ephesians 6:1-4 tells us:

> *Children, obey your parents in the Lord, for this is right. "Honor your father and mother"—which is the first commandment with a promise—"that it may go well with you and that you may enjoy long life on the earth." Fathers, do not exasperate your children; instead, bring them up in the training and instruction of the Lord.*

God commands children to obey the authorities that He's placed in their lives, namely their parents. To the obedient, He promises a long life. Children who honor their parents will be blessed by God here on earth.

Parents, too, must honor their children. They honor them by submitting to the needs of their children—bringing them up in the instruction of the Lord without discouraging them with unrealistic expectations (see Col. 3:21).

Many times young people have asked me if they should obey their parents when their parents—who are not Christians—ask them to do something that is not right in God's sight. Acts 5:29b tells us that "...*we must obey God rather than men!*"

If any authority in our lives asks us to do something that is sin, we need to obey God first! For example, Kako was a young Christian believer whose Buddhist parents wanted her to continue to attend and participate in their religious rituals. She could not obey her parents by continuing to worship these false gods and refused. God was her higher authority. Our obedience to any authority must always be based on a higher loyalty to God. So then, if parents or any other authority in our lives asks us to do anything that is against the Word of God, we need to obey God first.

SUBMIT TO EACH OTHER IN THE HOME

To be in submission is to be under the authority of the one responsible for the mission of our lives. At work, we are *under the mission* of our employer. In school, we are *under the mission* of our teacher. On a basketball team, we are *under the mission* of the coach. In the church, we are *under the mission* of the spiritual leadership that the Lord has placed in our lives. And in our homes, we are *under the mission* of the head of our home. Let's see how mutual submission is a principle applied to Christian families:

Submit to one another out of reverence for Christ. Wives, submit to your husbands as to the Lord. For the husband is the head of the wife as Christ is the head of the church, His body, of which He is the Savior (Ephesians 5:21-23).

In families, the Lord has called husbands and wives to submit to each other. God wants husbands and wives to be in unity as a team. However, in every team, there's always someone whom the Lord places as leadership in that team. In the case of the husband and wife, the Bible says that the husband is the head of the wife. His leadership must be exercised in love and consideration for his family. A husband has the responsibility to love his wife in the same way Jesus Christ loved His Church and gave His life for it (see Eph. 5:25).

As the leader in the home, a husband is responsible, in times of crisis, to make final decisions. A few years ago, my wife and I needed to make a decision about whether or not to send our children to a Christian school. We prayed and talked and prayed and talked, but finally we had to make a decision. My wife's response was that, as the head of the home, I needed to make the decision and that she would submit to my leadership. She trusted the Lord to lead me in making the right decision.

In a single parent home, the Lord gives special grace to moms and dads who do not have spouses to help them raise their children. The Bible says that our God is a father to the fatherless (see Ps. 68:5). The Lord also desires to use the Body of Christ (the local church) to assist moms and dads who are single parents (see James 1:27).

HONORING AUTHORITY IN THE CHURCH

The fourth area of authority that the Lord delegates to men and women is in the Church. Hebrews 13:17 says:

> *Obey your leaders and submit to their authority. They keep watch over you as men who must give an account. Obey them so that their work will be a joy, not a burden, for that would be of no advantage to you.*

The Lord places spiritual authorities in our lives who watch over us and who must give an account to the Lord for our spiritual lives. The Lord has placed elders and pastors in our lives to direct, correct, and protect us. That's why it's so important for every believer to be connected to the local church; it brings spiritual protection to us.

Paul was willing to be accountable to the spiritual leaders that the Lord had placed in his life. When Paul and Barnabas were sent out of the church of Antioch to plant churches throughout the world, they returned to their local church a few years later and reported all that the Lord had done (see Acts 14:27-28).

We should honor the spiritual leaders whom the Lord has placed in our lives according to First Thessalonians 5:12-13:

> *Now we ask you, brothers, to respect those who work hard among you, who are over you in the Lord and who admonish you. Hold them in the highest regard in love because of their work. Live in peace with each other.*

I meet people who say, "I don't agree with my pastor or my church leadership." I first encourage them to pray for God's blessing and wisdom on their spiritual leaders. After that, the Lord may also want them to appeal to their leaders in love about those issues, keeping in mind that they cannot change their leaders—that is God's responsibility. If the differences persist, they may also need to consider two other possibilities—maybe they have rebellion in their lives that they need to deal with, or perhaps the Lord has called them to another church.

Jesus, when teaching His disciples about leadership, instructed them to not be like the Gentiles who rule over others, but to be servants (see Matt. 20:25-28). Jesus was not suggesting that spiritual leaders have no responsibility or authority to give direction to the church, but that their attitude should be that of a servant. Spiritual authority and servanthood go hand-in-hand. For example, Nehemiah in the Old Testament, was a man of authority, but he did not lord it over the people like former governors (see Neh. 5:15). He was a servant who walked in the fear of the Lord.

The Lord's call on spiritual leaders is to help each believer draw closer to Jesus and learn from Him. The Lord has called us to have an attitude of submission toward the leaders whom He has placed in our lives. Years ago I heard a story of a little boy who insisted on standing on his chair during a church meeting. When his father took his hand and pulled him down into a seated position, the little boy looked up at his father and said, "I may be sitting down on the outside, but I'm standing up on the inside!" The Lord is concerned about our heart attitudes, and while "man looks on the outward appearance...the Lord looks at the heart" (1 Sam. 16:7).

To summarize, we are called to pray for, support, submit to, and appeal to our spiritual authorities. (We will talk more about appealing to authority in the next chapter.) Likewise, our spiritual authorities—pastors and elders—should pray for us, teach us, protect us, and correct us as we need it.

SIN IN A SPIRITUAL LEADER'S LIFE

What happens if a spiritual leader falls into sin? We should not blindly submit to a leader who has sin in his life but instead confront him according to First Timothy 5:19-20: *"Do not entertain an accusation against an elder unless it is brought by two or three witnesses. Those who sin are to be rebuked publicly, so that the others may take warning."*

If someone with spiritual authority (elder, pastor, cell group leader, house church leader, etc.) sins, and it is confirmed, those who are placed over the leader spiritually are responsible to discipline him or her. Most local churches are a part of a larger "family of churches" or a denomination. The leadership of this family of churches has the responsibility, along with the other elders, to administer proper discipline. In fact, the Bible says that a guilty senior leader should be rebuked in the presence of everyone in the church. This is why all leaders should also have spiritual authorities who will give them the direction, protection, and correction that they need as they serve the Lord in the local church.

If we have sin in our lives, the Lord instructs our church leaders to discipline us lovingly and restore us to walking in truth (see 1 Cor. 5, Gal. 6:1, Matt. 18:17). Loving earthly fathers will discipline their children in love because they care for their children. God has chosen to use people as His rod to discipline us (see 2 Sam. 7:14), but the discipline is to reclaim us, not to destroy us. Being disciplined shows that God loves us. In fact, the Lord tells us in Hebrews 12:8, *"If you are not disciplined (and everyone undergoes discipline), then you are illegitimate children and not true sons."*

As I stated previously, wherever you're committed in the Body of Christ—in a small group, a local congregation, or a house church—the Lord has called you to actively support and submit to the leadership that He has placed there. If someone makes an accusation against a leader, tell that person to go directly to the leader. Do not pass on gossip or accusations. Do not allow gossip or slander to hinder the work of God in your midst. And remember, the Lord has placed godly authorities in our lives to help mold us into the character of Jesus Christ.

DELEGATED AUTHORITY IN GOVERNMENT, WORKPLACE, FAMILY, AND CHURCH
REFLECTION QUESTIONS

1. Why should we be careful who we call a "whitewashed wall"? (See Acts 23:3.)

2. How are we really working for "employer" Jesus Christ on our jobs?

3. According to Acts 5:29, what should we do if an authority in our lives asks us to do something that is sinful?

4. What should happen if a leader has sin in his or her life (see 1 Tim. 5:19-20)? What should happen if we have sin in our lives?

Chapter 11

THE BLESSING
OF AUTHORITY

PROTECTION

In this chapter, we will look at some of the blessings that we receive when we submit to the authorities the Lord has placed in our lives. Some people grow up with a healthy understanding of honoring authority in their lives and realize that it is there for their protection. Others rebel against authority because they have an improper understanding of it. The Lord desires to renew our minds by His Word so that we can properly respect the delegated authorities He's placed in our lives.

First of all, submitting to authorities is a commandment of God:

> *Everyone must submit himself to the governing authorities, for there is no authority except that which God has established. The authorities that exist have been established by God. Consequently, he who rebels against the authority is rebelling against what God has instituted, and those who do so will bring judgment on themselves* (Romans 13:1-2).

Here the Scripture is talking about submitting to governing authorities, but it applies to all authorities in our lives. There is no authority except that which comes from God. In fact, God appoints the authorities that exist. In most cases, if we resist these authorities, we are resisting Him. We need to submit to the authorities that He's placed in our lives because these authorities give us protection.

For example, if we disobey the speed limit, we could be killed or kill someone else. If a parent tells a child not to play with matches and he disobeys, there could be the loss of a home or of a life. It would not be the parents' fault or God's fault; the child simply disobeyed the authority that was placed in his life. He moved out from under the umbrella of God's protection.

Having an attitude of submission toward the authorities whom God has placed in our lives will protect us from many mistakes. It also is a protection against the influence of the devil. The nature of the devil is rebellion and deceit. Lucifer fell from Heaven because he said, "I will be like the Most High." He refused to submit to God's authority.

In the universe there are two major forces—the one is submission to the authority of God; the other is rebellion. Whenever we allow an attitude of rebellion into our lives, we are beginning to be motivated by the enemy, which leads us to sin against God.

UNDERSTANDING PRINCIPLES OF FAITH

In order to be people of faith who see miracles happen in our lives, we must understand the principles of authority. When we submit to the authorities in our lives, we learn the principles of faith. The faith of the centurion in Matthew 8:8-10 was tied to his understanding of authority:

The centurion replied, "Lord, I do not deserve to have you come under my roof. But just say the word, and my servant will be healed. For I myself am a man under authority, with soldiers under me. I tell this one, 'Go,' and he goes; and that one, 'Come,' and he comes. I say to my servant, 'Do this,' and he does it.'' When Jesus heard this, He was astonished and said to those following Him, ''I tell you the truth, I have not found anyone in Israel with such great faith.''

This centurion received a miracle from Jesus because he understood authority. As an officer, he could issue orders to his subordinates, and they would obey. He completely understood that Christ, who possesses all authority, could give a command and that His will would be done.

When Jesus says a sickness must go, it must leave. His life on this earth was filled with examples of healing people of various sicknesses and diseases. The Scriptures teach us that we can expect miracles when we call for the elders of the church to pray for us if we are sick: *"He should call the elders of the church to pray...and the prayer offered in faith will make the sick person well..."* (James 5:14-15). The act of submitting to our spiritual leaders can release faith for healing in our lives.

CHARACTER TRAINING

Yet another blessing that we receive from learning to submit to the authorities in our lives is that it trains us in character to be a loving authority to others.

The Lord uses authorities in our lives who speak the Word of God to us. His Word chips away from our lives anything that is not from Him. Just as a blacksmith takes a piece of iron, makes it hot so that it becomes pliable, and then chips the impurities away with his hammer, God's Word purifies: *"'Is not my word like fire,' declares the Lord…"* (Jer. 23:29). It destroys all that is false in our lives and leaves only the genuine "metal." In the same way, our character is strengthened as we become conformed into the image of Christ.

God placed authorities in our lives to make us pliable. When we react to authority in anger and bitterness because we do not get our own way, it is probably a sign that there are still impurities that the Lord desires to chip away from our lives. The Word of God is a purifying fire that changes us more into His likeness.

If we haven't learned to submit to the authority in our lives in one setting, God will again bring someone into our new situation to whom we will have to learn to submit. He loves us that much. He is committed to seeing our lives motivated by the fruit of the Spirit: love, joy, peace, longsuffering, kindness, gentleness, goodness, faithfulness, and self-control (see Gal. 5:22-23).

GUIDANCE

We will also find that submitting to the authority that the Lord has placed in our lives often provides guidance for us to know His will. While growing up, my parents asked me to break off my relationship with certain ungodly friends. At the time, I did not appreciate what they were telling me. I felt controlled; but in retrospect, I am thankful to God for having submitted to their authority. I realize now that it saved me from having my life shipwrecked.

A contemporary Christian musician wanted to record an album; however, her parents asked her to wait. She found it difficult, but made a decision to submit to her parents. She later produced an album that has been a blessing to hundreds of thousands of people.

God blessed this musician and gave her the right timing for the release of her album.

Joseph, in the Old Testament, submitted to the authority of the jailer, even though he was falsely imprisoned. The Lord later raised him up as prime minister for the whole nation (see Gen. 39-40).

Jesus himself submitted to His heavenly Father every day. Jesus says in John 5:30b, "...*for I seek not to please Myself but Him who sent Me.*" Jesus was committed to walking in submission to His heavenly Father's authority. Jesus did nothing of his own initiative, but only that which was initiated by His heavenly Father.

WHAT IF THE AUTHORITY IS WRONG?

Many times people have asked me, "What should I do if the authority in my life is wrong?" As we mentioned before, we should obey God rather than man if the authority in our lives requires us to do something contrary to God's Word. But what if we believe the godly authority in our lives is making a mistake? Philippians 4:6 tells us to make an appeal: "*Do not be anxious about anything, but in everything, by prayer and petition, with thanksgiving, present your requests to God.*"

First of all, we need to appeal to God. We should pray, making known our requests and concerns, as we appeal to Him as our authority. This action sets a precedent for us to appeal to the delegated authorities in our lives. According to *Merriam-Webster's Dictionary*, the word *appeal* means "an earnest entreaty or a plea."[1] The Lord wants us to appeal to the authorities whom He has placed in our lives with an attitude of submission.

Instead of having a submissive spirit and appealing to authority, Aaron and Miriam accused Moses regarding the leadership decisions that He was making. They did not fear God or respect God's prophet, and this allowed a spirit of rebellion to come into their lives. Moses, who had learned his lesson about authority in the desert while herding sheep, did not defend himself. Instead he went to God, and God defended him (see Num. 12).

Daniel and his friends, in the Old Testament, appealed to the authority in their lives and asked only to eat certain foods (see Dan. 1:8,12-13). The Lord honored their appeal to authority and blessed them with health, wisdom, literary skill, and supernatural revelation.

Nehemiah appealed to the king to take a trip to Jerusalem (see Neh. 2:4-5). His appeal to the authority in his life in an attitude of submission caused the king to grant his request. Nehemiah's attitude and obedience made it possible for the wall to be built around Jerusalem.

If any person in authority in our lives requires us to sin, we must obey God and not man (see Acts 5:29). The early Church leaders were told by the religious leaders of their day to stop proclaiming Jesus as Lord. They could not obey these orders, but they still maintained a spirit and attitude of honoring the religious leaders. If the authorities in our lives are asking us to cheat, steal, lie, or sin in any way, we must obey the living God first. However, this is rarely the case. Usually God uses the authorities in our lives to help mold and structure our lives for good.

AN ATTITUDE OF LOVE AND SUBMISSION

God's concern is that we have an attitude of love and submission to our God and to those He's placed in authority in our lives. This is often opposite of what we see today—people are more concerned about being right in their own eyes and insist on "doing their own thing."

Korah was a priest in the Old Testament who rose up in rebellion against Moses with 250 other leaders in Israel. Rather than appealing in love and submission to Moses' and Aaron's authority, they challenged their authority:

> *They came as a group to oppose Moses and Aaron and said to them, "You have gone too far! The whole community is holy, every one of them, and the Lord is with them. Why then do you set yourselves above the Lord's assembly?"* (Numbers 16:3)

Korah and the other leaders were rebellious. They thought they could choose for themselves who would lead God's people. But God made it certain; He was in charge. The next day, the ground opened up and swallowed all of them alive. God hates rebellion.

Abigail, in First Samuel 25, realized that David and his army were coming to destroy her husband and their people. She went to David and appealed to him, and he honored her; Abigail's wise appeal kept David from harming her family—and from avenging himself with his own hands (see 1 Sam. 25:33).

A friend of mine was required to sign a job-related document but realized that the technical wording would make him sign an untruth. He prayed and decided that he needed to obey God. Before he went to his supervisors to appeal to them, he asked the Lord for wisdom to fulfill his employer's intentions without compromising the truth. The Lord showed him a plan, but he was prepared to give up his job if required.

He told his supervisors that he appreciated working at the company and explained why he could not sign the document. He admitted that it might inconvenience them or that he could lose his job; still, he needed to be faithful to God and not tell a lie. On his own time, he volunteered to change the format of the document so that it legally fulfilled their company's purpose at the same time. They accepted his idea, and the Lord gave him tremendous favor in that company.

UNDERSTANDING DELEGATED AUTHORITY

Some time back, a missionary in a South American nation was teaching a Sunday school class on the subject of authority from Romans 13. A doctor stood up and said, "Do you mean that I must pay the taxes that my government requires?" At that time, this nation had a very ineffective tax collection system. Less than 25 percent of the entire population paid taxes. The government realized this, so they raised the quota to four times more than what it should have been to cover the expenses for those who did not pay.

Convicted of this biblical principle, the doctor made a decision that day to pay his taxes, but he also prayed and asked the Lord for wisdom. The Lord gave the doctor an idea about how to change the tax collection system. He shared his new idea with the city officials, and they adopted his suggestion. It worked so well that 80 percent of the people started paying their taxes. The state then adopted the plan which was later adopted by the whole nation. The entire nation was blessed through one man's obedience. Let us dare to obey the Word of God and see what He does through our obedience.

When we understand the principle of God's delegated authority, it changes the way we think. Paul the apostle clearly understood delegated authority. God had given Paul delegated authority, so Paul delegated some of the Lord's authority to Timothy and sent him to the Christians at Corinth: *"For this reason I am sending to you Timothy, my son whom I love, who is faithful in the Lord. He will remind you of my way of life in Christ Jesus, which agrees with what I teach everywhere in every church"* (1 Cor. 4:17).

Years earlier, Paul, (then named Saul), was on the road to Damascus and blinded by a bright light. The Lord had instructed him to go into the city and have Ananias pray for him. Paul did not say, "But I want Peter, the apostle, to pray for me, or James." He was willing to receive prayer from the servant the Lord had chosen. Consequently, he was filled with the Holy Spirit and received his sight. Ananias probably was an "unknown" Christian in the Church world at that time, but both Paul and Ananias understood the principle of God's delegated authority, and God honored them both. Similarly, when we honor God's delegated authority, God will honor us—this is part of our maturing process as we, in turn, become sons and daughters to whom God can delegate authority.

ENDNOTE

1. *Merriam-Webster's Collegiate Dictionary*, 11th ed., s.v. "Appeal."

THE BLESSING OF AUTHORITY
REFLECTION QUESTIONS

1. What can submitting to authority teach us about faith?

2. How is God's Word shaping you? What is the Lord chipping away from your life? Which of the fruit(s) of the Spirit is it being replaced with?

3. Have you ever submitted to an authority in your life and discovered God's will for your life as a result?

4. What is often the result of appealing to authority? What is the result of rebellion?

Chapter 12

THE BLESSING OF ACCOUNTABILITY

WHAT IS PERSONAL ACCOUNTABILITY?

Accountability is giving an account to others for what God has called us to do. We are first accountable to the Lord regarding how we live out our commitment to Christ. Our lives need to line up with the Word of God. Then we are accountable to fellow believers. These people are often the spiritual leaders whom God has placed in our lives. Hebrews 13:17 says that these leaders are accountable to God concerning us because they *"...keep watch over you as men who must give an account...."*

Many times I've asked others to keep me accountable for a goal that I believe the Lord has set for me. Several years ago, I asked one of the men in a Bible study group in which I was involved to hold me accountable with my personal time in prayer and in meditating in God's Word each day. Every morning at 7:00 A.M. I received a phone call as my friend checked up on me. Accountability enabled me to be victorious. There is a tremendous release that happens in our lives when we are willing to ask others to hold us accountable for what the Lord has shown us for certain personal areas that need encouragement and support.

I want to emphasize that personal accountability is not having others tell us what to do. Personal accountability is finding out from God what He wants us to do and then asking others to hold us accountable to do those things. Spiritual abuse can occur when someone in a position of spiritual authority in our lives misuses that authority and attempts to control us. This is not biblical accountability! The purpose of authority is to help build us up. If someone's seemingly "godly" accountability attempts to manipulate us rather than free us to do what God has called us to do, it is a misuse of power.

ACCOUNTABLE TO JESUS FIRST

As we just mentioned, we are first accountable to the Lord as to how we live out our commitment to Him. Mark 6 shows how the 12 disciples were accountable to Jesus. He had trained them, and now they were ready to be sent out on a task. In verse 7, Jesus sends them out two by two so that they could comfort and support each other in their mission: "*Calling the Twelve to Him, He sent them out two by two and gave them authority over evil spirits.*"

After they had ministered, verse 30 says that the disciples reported back to Jesus what they had experienced. This is an example of accountability in operation: "*The apostles gathered around Jesus and reported to Him all they had done and taught*" (Mark 6:30).

Another time, when 72 disciples were sent out, they also came back and were accountable to Jesus. Luke 10:1,17 tells us, "*After this the Lord appointed seventy-two others and sent them two by two ahead of Him to every town and place where He was about to go....The seventy-two returned with joy and said, 'Lord, even the demons submit to us in Your name.'*"

If the early disciples needed to be accountable to Jesus, the One who had sent them out, how much more we need to be accountable to our Lord Jesus Christ. We are accountable by living our lives in obedience to God's Word as we put our hope in His promises (see Ps. 119:74) and hide it deep within our hearts (see Ps. 119:11).

ACCOUNTABLE TO OTHERS

We are often faced with serious spiritual battles that we must learn to overcome. Others can help us face those battles. Accountability consists of someone loving us enough to check up on us so that we can stay on track in our personal lives. Paul wrote to the Roman Christians to remind them of the truths that they already knew. He wanted to encourage them to correct and hold each other accountable in a loving way: *"Now I myself am confident concerning you, my brethren, that you also are full of goodness, filled with all knowledge, able also to admonish one another"* (Rom. 15:14 NKJV).

According to *Merriam-Webster's Dictionary, admonish* means "to express warning or disapproval to especially in a gentle, earnest, or solicitous manner; to give friendly earnest advice or encouragement to."[1] We all need people in our lives to admonish us and hold us accountable. It doesn't just happen. We need to ask. *"God opposes the proud, but gives grace to the humble"* (1 Pet. 5:5b). It takes humility to ask others to hold us accountable for the way that we live our Christian lives, but God gives grace to those who are humble and willing to open their lives to others.

One time, after spending a few days praying with a group of Christian leaders, I asked one of the fellow leaders to hold me accountable for the way that I conducted myself as a Christian leader. He consented and asked me to do the same for him. There is tremendous freedom and protection in being accountable to someone else. The devil dwells in darkness and will try to isolate us from other believers. Jesus desires for us to walk in the light of openness and accountability.

STANDING UNDER TEMPTATION

Many times a Christian will begin to grow in his Christian life and then fall back into a mediocre Christian experience. Other times believers are overtaken by temptation and fall into sin. Accountability to another person helps us to stay on fire for God and to stand up under temptation: *"…God is faithful; He will not let you be tempted beyond what you can bear. But when you are tempted, He will also provide a way out so that you can stand up under it"* (1 Cor. 10:13).

We should not be afraid to be honest about our struggles and shortfalls. One of the benefits of accountability is that often we find that we are not the only one who struggles in a particular area. Knowing that we are not alone with our problems helps us to admit our weaknesses so that we can be healed: *"Therefore confess your sins to each other and pray for each other so that you may be healed"* (James 5:16).

Who are the people the Lord has placed in your life? Ask them to hold you accountable to do what the Lord has called you to do. Perhaps you need accountability in handling your finances properly. Or perhaps you need to be accountable for how you relate to your spouse.

If you desire to lose weight, you'll find a tremendous blessing in being accountable to someone for your eating habits and daily exercise. I once heard a man say that he had lost over 20,000 pounds in his lifetime. He would lose a few pounds and then gain the weight back, lose it again, then gain it back again. The cycle went on and on. Although he was exaggerating and joking about his physical condition, the truth is, he desperately needed to be accountable to someone in his life. Accountability is freeing! It encourages us to move on to maturity and victory in our lives.

Accountability keeps us from becoming lazy in our relationship with the Lord and provides a "way out" for us when temptation hits. The Bible tells us to encourage one another daily so that we do not become hardened by sin's deceitfulness (see Heb. 3:13).

HELP WITH OUR "BLIND SPOTS"

Many drivers experience what we call a "blind spot" while passing, turning, or backing up their vehicle. In this potentially dangerous blind spot, it is impossible to see oncoming traffic.

In the same way, many of us have blind spots in our lives that we often miss but that others can see. There are many people in our lives who can help us with the blind spots. These people can hold us accountable as to how we are living our lives. At work, we may be accountable to a foreman. In the home, husbands and wives are accountable to one another. Children are accountable to their parents. We are accountable to the leaders in our church. The Scriptures tell us in Proverbs 11:14, "...*in the multitude of counselors there is safety*" (NKJV). A friend of mine once said, "Learn to listen to your critics. They may tell you things that your friends may never tell you." This is good advice.

Something to remember when we hold others accountable is that we should not judge their attitudes. Instead, we help them see certain actions in their lives that may be displeasing to the Lord. We should speak it in a way that will encourage them. We are accountable for the words we speak: *"But I tell you that men will have to give account on the day of judgment for every careless word they have spoken. For by your words you will be acquitted, and by your words you will be condemned"* (Matt. 12:36-37).

At one point in my Christian life, I was convicted by the Lord to develop a more intimate relationship with Him. I shared honestly about this need in my life with one of the men in my small group. There were certain things that I knew I needed to do to pursue my relationship with Jesus, and this Christian friend "checked up on me" or held me accountable by encouraging me to do them.

Matthew 18 describes a slightly different scenario of accountability in the Church. When a professing Christian brother or sister sins against us privately, what should we do to hold them accountable to that sin? This Scripture says that we should not go to someone else about the problem. We must love the offender enough to go directly to him. If he has sin in his life and does not receive you, the Bible says that we should then take one or two Christian friends along and talk to him again (see Matt. 18:15-17). The goal is to see him restored and healed.

The goal of accountability is always to reach out in love and humility to an individual so that he receives a reaffirmation of God's love in his life and is restored to Christlikeness.

ACCOUNTABILITY IN A SMALL GROUP

God did not create us to live without fellowshipping with other believers. When it comes to the everyday experience of living for

Jesus, we need people in our lives with whom we are in close relationship to encourage us.

> *And let us consider how we may spur one another on toward love and good deeds. Let us not give up meeting together, as some are in the habit of doing, but let us encourage one another—and all the more as you see the Day approaching* (Hebrews 10:24-25).

> *If one falls down, his friend can help him up. But pity the man who falls and has no one to help him up!* (Ecclesiastes 4:10)

Fellow believers can help to keep us accountable to those things that the Lord is saying to us. A small group of believers in a Sunday School class, a small group, a youth group, or a house church can be a great community within which to express the desire for accountability. We cannot be accountable to everyone in a large setting, but in a small group of people, we can more easily share our struggles and receive the help we need to overcome a problem or temptation.

In a small group, we can be trained, equipped, and encouraged in the things of God. No one should try to live his or her Christian life without the support of others. We can save ourselves much heartache by learning the principle of accountability and applying it to our lives within a small group.

OUR ULTIMATE AUTHORITY IS JESUS

Our ultimate authority and accountability must come from Jesus, not from other people. Jesus gives us His authority to live victorious lives: *"I have given you authority to trample on snakes and scorpions and to overcome all the power of the enemy; nothing will harm you"* (Luke 10:19).

Jesus is the One from whom we receive authority. Even though God uses delegated authorities in our lives and requires us to have an attitude of submission to them, God is the one who gives us ultimate authority. We even have authority over the demons in Jesus' name because of the authority of Jesus Christ. When we receive that authority by knowing Him and living in an intimate relationship with Jesus, His Word gives us authority.

When Jesus spoke, people listened. As we draw close to Jesus, we also will speak with the authority of Jesus Christ: *"When Jesus had finished saying these things, the crowds were amazed at His teaching, because He taught as one who had authority, and not as their teachers of the law"* (Matt. 7:28-29).

In summary, God is restoring the fear of the Lord in our generation. He has called us to submit to the authorities whom He's placed in our lives. As we submit to these authorities, the Lord teaches us the principles of faith. The Lord gives authority to His delegated authorities to mold, shape, and form us into the image of Christ. These authorities are found in governments, places of work, in our families, in our communities, and in our church.

The Lord has called us to have an attitude of submission to the authorities whom He's placed in our lives, realizing that ultimate authority is His. We should never obey any authority that is causing us to sin (see Acts 5:29). We must obey God rather than man. If we believe the authorities in our lives are causing us to sin, we need to pray and then appeal to them.

Who are the authorities that the Lord has placed in your life? Who is holding you accountable? A proper understanding of authority and accountability brings tremendous security and freedom to us. Knowing that the Lord loves us enough to place authorities in our lives to protect us and to mold us is wonderful. Knowing that the people the Lord has placed in our lives love us enough to hold us accountable with our actions is a tremendous blessing. We do not have to live our Christian lives alone. God bless you as you experience the loving authority of Jesus Christ and the blessing of accountability.

ENDNOTE

1. *Merriam-Webster's Collegiate Dictionary*, 11th ed., s.v. "Admonish."

THE BLESSING OF ACCOUNTABILITY
REFLECTION QUESTIONS

1. Who "keeps watch over you"? Give an example of personal accountability from your own life.

2. Have you ever humbled yourself to ask another person to hold you accountable? What happened? How has God used other people to help you stand up under temptation?

3. Have you ever helped someone else be accountable to God?

4. According to Hebrews 10:24-25, why is it important to fellowship with other believers?

PART IV

God's Perspective on Finances

Chapter 13

WE ARE MANAGERS
OF GOD'S MONEY

GOD LOVES A CHEERFUL GIVER

God wants to bless us financially! John 3:16 says that *"...God so loved the world that He **gave**..."* God introduced Himself to Abraham in Genesis 17:1 as *El Shaddai*...the God of *more than enough*.[1] He met Abraham's needs and provided abundantly for Abraham to bless the nations. God desires to meet our needs and provide abundantly for us to minister to others.

Many Christians have an unhealthy understanding of finances. They may give out of a sense of duty or obligation. Giving should come out of a sense of faith in God's grace (2 Cor. 8:1-4); it should never be done grudgingly or out of a sense of compulsion: *"Each man should give what he has decided in his heart to give, not reluctantly or under compulsion, for God loves a cheerful giver"* (2 Cor. 9:7). A Christian friend of mine visited a non-believing friend one weekend and asked his friend to attend church with him. My friend recalls how embarrassed he was when he realized that the purpose of the service that Sunday morning was to collect money to purchase a new organ. They began to ask for pledges—$1,000 pledges, $500 pledges, and $100 pledges. In fact, it took the entire meeting to prod and beg the people to make pledges. The non-Christian friend was so disillusioned by what he experienced that he never wanted to return to church!

Scripture has much to say about money and material possessions. Sixteen of the 38 parables of Jesus deal with money. One out of every ten verses in the New Testament addresses this subject. Scripture has 500 verses on prayer, less than 500 verses on faith, but over 2,000 verses on the subject of money and material possessions.[2] Money is such an important issue because a person's attitude toward it often is revealing of his or her relationship with God.

God wants to restore a healthy, godly understanding of finances in the Body of Christ today. Let's be open to what God's Word says about finances.

WE ARE MANAGERS ONLY

First and foremost, we must realize that everything we have belongs to God. We are merely stewards (managers) of any material goods that we possess. God owns everything that we have, but He makes us managers of it:

> *Let a man so consider us, as servants of Christ and stewards of the mysteries of God. Moreover it is required in stewards that one be found faithful....And what do you have that you did not receive...* (1 Corinthians 4:1-2,7b NKJV).

When my wife, LaVerne, and I served as missionaries, we had the job of buying the food and supplies for the other missionaries at our base each week. The money we were using was not our own; we were simply managing it. It belonged to the mission board.

I shared this principle of being a manager of God's money in Nairobi, Kenya, one time, and it made complete sense to one of the ladies in the audience. She told me that, as a bank teller, she understood that even though she handles massive amounts of money daily, the money is not hers. It belongs to the bank. She is simply a manager.

I am a manager of the Lord's money. In reality, the money in my wallet is not mine; it is God's. Some Christians believe that 10 percent of the money they receive is God's and that the other 90 percent belongs exclusively to them. They are mistaken. It *all* belongs to God. We need to recognize His ownership in everything that we have.

…For everything in heaven and earth is Yours….wealth and honor come from You… (1 Chronicles 29:11b-12a).

"The silver is Mine and the gold is Mine," declares the Lord Almighty (Haggai 2:8).

For every animal of the forest is Mine, and the cattle on a thousand hills (Psalm 50:10).

While LaVerne and I served as missionaries, I drove a van owned by the mission, and although I sensed responsibility for the van, I realized that it did not belong to me. Ultimately, it belonged to God. It was a good lesson in managing someone else's property—similar to the responsibility that we have to manage the wealth that God gives us. God has given us a responsibility as managers of His wealth. It all belongs to Him. We have to stop thinking like owners and start thinking like managers.

WE CANNOT SERVE GOD AND MONEY

Did you know that God associates our ability to handle money with our ability to handle spiritual matters? One day Jesus made some amazing statements regarding this principle:

> *Whoever can be trusted with very little can also be trusted with much, and whoever is dishonest with very little will also be dishonest with much. So if you have not been trustworthy in handling worldly wealth, who will trust you with true riches? And if you have not been trustworthy with someone else's property, who will give you property of your own? No servant can serve two masters. Either he will hate the one and love the other, or he will be devoted to the one and despise the other. You cannot serve both God and Money* (Luke 16:10-13).

Money, in terms of true value, is a "little" thing. However, faithfulness in little things (money) indicates our faithfulness in big things (spiritual values). Jesus said that those who are not trustworthy in the use of their worldly wealth will be the same with spiritual things. Jesus said that we cannot serve two masters—God and materialism. It is impossible to hold allegiance to two masters at the same time.

Being surrounded with the world's riches may give us a false sense of security. Christians must not hold on too tightly to possessions because they have a way of deceiving us and demanding our hearts' loyalty. How we handle finances often is a reflection or indicator of our hearts. The Lord is very concerned with our use of finances because He knows that, if He can trust us with finances, He can trust us with spiritual things.

WE SHOULD EXPECT FINANCIAL BLESSINGS

It amazes me to see how God constantly takes risks on His creation. When God created the angels, He took a risk. The archangel, lucifer (satan), tried to exalt himself above the Lord, so God had to throw him out of Heaven (see Isa. 14:12-17). When God created mankind, giving us free will, He took a risk.

Did you know that every time God blesses us financially, He is taking a risk? He takes a risk with you and me when He asks us to be stewards (managers) of His finances and material possessions because we may begin to serve money instead of serving the true God. God, at times, blessed Israel with wealth as a sign that He was fulfilling His covenant: *"But remember the Lord your God, for it is He who gives you the ability to produce wealth..."* (Deut. 8:18). We should expect financial blessings from the Lord. God wants us to be fruitful.

However, with the blessing of wealth, the Lord instructed His people to be careful so that they would not forget the Lord their God. God knows that our tendency is to allow money to be our god. We must remember that our lives do not consist in the abundance of the things that we possess: *"...Watch out! Be on your guard against all kinds of greed; a man's life does not consist in the abundance of his possessions"* (Luke 12:15).

In the first of the Ten Commandments, the Lord commands us to have no other gods before Him (see Exod. 20:3). The last commandment says that we should not covet what belongs to our neighbors (see Exod. 20:17). To *covet* means "to feel inordinate desire for what belongs to another."[3] If we covet others' financial blessings, we are putting money ahead of God. Material possessions do not give life to us. Only a relationship with Jesus produces life. We must not allow material wealth to distract us from our heavenly calling.

IS IT BETTER TO BE RICH OR POOR?

Christians may fall into one of two camps when it comes to what they believe is God's perspective regarding a Christian's financial lifestyle—some may take the viewpoint that all Christians should be poor, and others may take the viewpoint that all Christians should be rich.

Those who believe that all Christians should be rich often believe financial wealth is a clear sign of God's blessing. However, God's blessing cannot *always* be equated with personal material gain. It involves so much more. God certainly wants to bless us financially. He wants to bless us in every way: *"Dear friend, I pray that you may enjoy good health and that all may go well with you, even as your soul is getting along well"* (3 John 1:2).

However, if we believe, like the Pharisees did, that great wealth is a *sign* of God's favor, we will look down on people who are poor. The Pharisees looked down on Jesus for being financially poor (see Luke 16:14). But Jesus did not do the same. In fact, we see that the people of the church at Smyrna were destitute, yet Jesus said that they were spiritually rich (see Rev. 2:8-10). Although God wants to prosper us in every way, including financially, financial wealth does not necessarily mean that we are blessed by God. The Laodicean Christians were a case in point. Scripture tells us they were wealthy, yet they were considered spiritually "wretched" (see Rev. 3:17).

On the other hand, many wealthy people *are* blessed by God because they use their finances unselfishly. Job was a rich and godly man who did not allow his money to become his god (see Job 1).

Abraham also had great wealth and was very godly (see Gen. 13:2). Before he had an encounter with Jesus, Zacchaeus, a wealthy tax collector, trusted his riches instead of trusting in the living God. But after he met Jesus, he gave back four times what he had taken from others (see Luke 19:8).

In the other camp, and often in reaction to the very seductive power of money in our lives, some believers take the viewpoint that all Christians should be poor. They often have a fear of what money can do to them. They fear its corrupting influence and believe money will cause them to backslide. Some may have been wounded by financial scandals in the Church and now reject any kind of wealth as having an evil influence.

Cutting through the smoke of the two opposing viewpoints, the truth is this: the Lord is not for or against money; it has no morality to Him. Money is amoral in and of itself. It is *what we do with it* and *our attitude toward it* that makes it moral or immoral. Money is not the root of evil, like some people like to misquote in First Timothy 6:10. In this Scripture, the Lord warns us to beware of the pitfall of *loving* money. It is the *love* of money that is a root of all kinds of evil: *"For the love of money is a root of all kinds of evil. Some people, eager for money, have wandered from the faith and pierced themselves with many griefs"* (1 Tim. 6:10).

We can be lovers of money, whether we have little or much. It depends on what we are placing our affections in. Rich or poor, if we begin to love money, it will lead us down the path of greed and cause much pain in our lives and in the lives of those around us.

GIVING PREVENTS MATERIALISM

Although God wants to bless us materially, it should not be our focus: *"People who want to get rich fall into temptation and a trap and into many foolish and harmful desires that plunge men into ruin and destruction"* (1 Tim. 6:9).

The Lord does not want us to have money on our minds all the time. Materialism is a preoccupation with material rather than spiritual things. Our primary focus should be on the Kingdom of God, not on money. However, it does take money to expand the Kingdom of God. We should not be a slave to money because God's purpose for money is for it to be a servant to us. Money is for purchasing the necessities of life, giving to those in need, and financing the spread of the Kingdom of God. This bears repeating: the real purpose for receiving God's prosperity is to expand the Kingdom of God.

Giving keeps us from materialism. Giving breaks the power of money to become an idol in our lives. God wants to bless us so that we can sow into His Kingdom and help the poor.

To be blessed financially simply means that we have all that we need to meet the needs in our lives and an abundance left over to give to others. The purpose for having a job and working should be for *"...doing something useful with* [our] *own hands, that* [we] *may have something to share with those in need"* (Eph. 4:28b).

When we diligently work and faithfully give of our finances, the Bible teaches that God *"will meet all* [our] *needs according to His glorious riches"* (Phil. 4:19). He wants to meet our needs and enable us to meet the needs of others. God promises to take care of us. He wants to bless and prosper us. Whether you are a businessman, an employee, a student, or a housewife, the Lord desires to prosper you. Remember, God revealed Himself to Abraham as *El Shaddai*...the

God of more than enough. He promised to bless Abraham abundantly, just as He desires to meet our needs and abundantly bless us in every way today. Giving really does keep us from becoming materialistic.

GIVE SACRIFICIALLY

In Luke 21, Jesus gives a lesson on how God evaluates giving. Jesus and His disciples were watching people place their gifts into the temple treasury. The rich put in large amounts of money because they could easily spare it, but then a poor widow dropped two small coins in the treasury. She gave all that she possibly could, and it required great personal sacrifice. Jesus remarked that the poor widow put in more than all the others because of the amount of sacrifice it required of her.

It is not the amount that we give, but the sacrifice that is involved. When we give out of a heart of love and compassion for others, we will discover that God will take care of our own needs and more! As we give generously, God promises:

> *...to make all grace abound to you, so that in all things at all times, having all that you need, you will abound in every good work...Now He who supplies seed to the sower and bread for food will also supply and increase your store of seed and will enlarge the harvest of your righteousness. You will be made rich in every way so that you can be generous on every occasion, and through us your generosity will result in thanksgiving to God"* (2 Corinthians 9:8,10-11).

You can give either sparingly or generously. You are rewarded accordingly: *"...with the measure you use, it will be measured you"*

(Matt. 7:2). When you give sacrificially, God resupplies what you have given and increases your giving capacity. The more you give, the more you are blessed, and the more you can give. God wants to bless you financially so that you have enough for yourself and enough to share with others.

ENDNOTES

1. "Names of God in Judaism," Wikipedia, http://en.wikipedia.org/wiki/Names_of_God_in_Judaism#Shaddai (accessed 16 Sept 2008).

2. J. Hampton Keathley, "Financial Faithfulness," Bible.org, www.bible.org/page.php?page_id=813 (accessed 15 Sept 2008).

3. *Merriam-Webster's Collegiate Dictionary*, 11th ed., s.v. "Covet."

WE ARE MANAGERS OF GOD'S MONEY
REFLECTION QUESTIONS

1. Why does God want to bless us financially?

2. Have you ever been entrusted with another person's money or possessions? How did you feel about those things?

3. Why is God taking a risk by making us managers of His finances?

4. Recall some instances when you gave sacrificially and God took care of your needs.

Chapter 14

THE
TITHE

GIVING A PORTION OF OUR INCOME

The Lord gives us the responsibility of managing the resources that He gives to us. He has set up a system to constantly remind us of His ownership in everything. This systematic way to give is a first step to allowing our resources to be used for God's Kingdom. In the Old Testament, the Israelites were required to give one-tenth of all their income to the Lord. The Hebrew word for *tithe* means "a tenth part."[1] At the very heart of tithing is the idea that God owns everything. God was simply asking the Israelites to return what He first gave them: *"Honor the Lord with your wealth, with the first-fruits of all your crops; then your barns will be filled to overflowing, and your vats will brim over with new wine"* (Prov. 3:9-10).

We honor God by giving Him the "firstfruits," or a portion, of our income. It shows that we honor Him as the Lord of all of our possessions. This tithe (ten percent) opens up a way for God to pour out His blessings on us. Every time we give our tithes, we are reminded that all of our money and earthly possessions belong to God. We are simply stewards responsible for what the Lord has given us. The word *tithe* is first mentioned in Genesis 14:18-20:

Then Melchizedek king of Salem brought out bread and wine. He was priest of God Most High, and he blessed Abram, saying, "Blessed be Abram by God Most High, Creator of heaven and earth. And blessed be God Most High, who delivered your enemies into your hand." Then Abram gave him a tenth of everything.

Abraham gave Melchizedek a tithe before the Old Testament law had even been written. Abraham was honoring the Lord and Melchizedek as the priest of the Most High God with ten percent of that which the Lord had given to him. He may have learned this principle from Abel who brought the firstborn of his flock to the Lord.

At the end of every month, I face a stack of bills that I need to pay. One of these bills is my bill to God. It is called a *tithe*, my "first-fruit." This tithe reminds me that everything that I have belongs to Him. I have learned to enjoy returning this ten percent to the Lord. After all, Jesus has given to me 100 percent of Himself through His death on the cross. I am eternally grateful!

DON'T TRY TO STEAL FROM GOD

In the 1992 riots in Los Angeles, California, looting took place in many stores and businesses. A young man was asked by a reporter what he had stolen. He said, "I stole Christian tapes because I am a Christian." You might think that sounds ridiculous. Yet, in a similar way, there are many Christians who are stealing from God by keeping for themselves that which really belongs to the Lord—the tithe.

In Old Testament history, some of the Israelites were robbing God by selfishly holding onto money that belonged to God. They were required to give at least one-tenth of the livestock, the land's produce, and their income to the Lord. In addition, they were required to bring other offerings in the form of sacrifices or free-will offerings. But God says they were holding back:

"Will a man rob God? Yet you have robbed Me! But you say, 'In what way have we robbed You?' In tithes and offerings. You are cursed with a curse, for you have robbed Me, even this whole nation. Bring all the tithes into the storehouse, that there may be food in My house, and try Me now in this," says the Lord of hosts, "If I will not open for you the windows of heaven and pour out for you such blessing that there will not be room enough to receive it. And I will rebuke the devourer for your sakes, so that he will not destroy the fruit of your ground, nor shall the vine fail to bear fruit for you in the field," says the Lord of hosts (Malachi 3:8-11 NKJV).

When the people asked God how they were robbing Him, He responded clearly, "In tithes and offerings." Notice, He not only tells us to bring tithes, but also offerings. We'll talk more about offerings in the next chapter.

Many of God's people today are robbing God in this same way. The Lord has promised us that, if we obey Him and bring all of our tithes into the storehouse, He will open the windows of Heaven, pour out a blessing on us, and "rebuke the devourer." Many people are struggling financially because the devil has been robbing and devouring them. The enemy has not been rebuked by the Lord because they are not paying tithes into the storehouse.

We are blessed as God rebukes the devourer when we tithe. However, our primary motivation for tithing should not be to get something back from God. Our primary motivation for tithing is obedience—to God and His Word.

I've known some people who have said that, when they initially began to tithe, the enemy attacked them, and they found themselves worse off financially than ever before. The enemy may test us when we obey the Word of God. When Jesus was baptized, the heavens opened, and the Lord said, "This is my beloved Son in whom I am well pleased" (see Matt. 3:17 NKJV). During the next 40 days of His life, Jesus was tested by the enemy. Tests will always come; however, if we hold on, we will receive the blessing that comes from obedience. God's promises always prove to be true!

When I was a missionary, the enemy tested me in the area of tithing. "You gave your entire life to God," he told me, "how could the Lord expect you to give back a tithe from the small amount of money that you are receiving?" By the grace of God, I refused the enemy's lies and began to tithe on even the small amount that the Lord had provided for us. The Lord blessed us over and over again in a supernatural way as we served in the mission field. God is faithful. He honors His Word.

THE TITHE IS A BILL TO GOD

The tithe is a numerical expression reminding us that all that we have belongs to God. Some years ago, I was reading the Book of Malachi and was convicted by the Lord in the area of tithing. I checked my bank ledger. I had a whole list of bills. In fact, one of the bills that I was delinquent in paying was my bill to God. Every month, my bill to God grew. I was not paying my tithe because I thought I did not have enough money to pay it.

One day, I made a decision to obey God. When I received my next paycheck, I paid all of my tithes to God. Some time later, I realized that something supernatural had happened after I took this step of obedience. Our money seemed to last longer! The Lord began to provide for us financially, often in supernatural ways. It didn't happen overnight, but God began to bless us in a new way, and the devourer was rebuked.

Some people say, "I can't afford to tithe." The truth is—they cannot afford to withhold the tithe. A tithe is money set apart for God. If we don't give it to God, the devourer will consume it. Let's read again what God says in His Word about rebuking the devourer when we give tithes and offerings into His storehouse: *"And I will rebuke the devourer for your sakes, so that he will not destroy the fruit of your ground, nor shall the vine fail to bear fruit for you in the field…"* (Mal. 3:11 NKJV).

The word *devour* in the original Hebrew text means "to eat, burn up or consume."[2] During the days of Malachi, God's people were experiencing famine, scarcity, unseasonable weather, and insects that ate up the fruits of the earth. According to the above Scripture, the enemy will devour our blessings when we choose not to obey God's principles. When we walk out from under the umbrella of protection that results from obedience to the Word of God concerning tithing, we give the enemy a legal right to devour our blessings.

According to *Merriam-Webster's Dictionary*, to *tithe* is "to pay or give a tenth part of especially for the support of the church."[3] When you pay your taxes to the government, do you *feel* like paying it? Do we have to *feel* like paying our tithe back to God? Of course not. Whether or not we *feel* like tithing is not the issue. We need to tithe in *obedience* to Him.

Imagine going to the bank and paying off a loan or a mortgage. How does the bank teller respond when we pay? Does she pat us on the back and tell us how much she appreciates it that we came to pay our bill? No, and neither should we expect God to pat us on the back when we tithe. We are not doing God any great favor when we tithe. It belongs to Him anyway. It is our responsibility to tithe, and we do it out of obedience.

GIVING SYSTEMATICALLY

The Lord wants us to learn to give systematically just like the believers were encouraged to do in First Corinthians 16:2: *"On the first day of every week, each one of you should set aside a sum of money in keeping with his income, saving it up, so that when I come no collections will have to be made."*

Some believers claim to "follow the Spirit" as to when they will tithe. That's like calling your electric company and saying, "I'm not sure if I will pay my bill this month. Maybe I'll pay it next month. I'm just going to follow the Spirit." If you did not pay, you would get your electric service disconnected. We should always follow the Holy Spirit within the framework of the Word of God. The Word of God teaches us to tithe systematically as an act of obedience, not just when we feel like it.

Imagine giving your employer a phone call and telling him, "I will come to work when I think the Spirit is prompting me to come." Guess what would happen? You would probably lose your job! The same principle applies to giving to the Lord in a systematic way. Yes, we should follow the Spirit in our giving that is over and above our regular tithes. However, our God is a God of order and discipline. He instructs us to give tithes systematically so that we do not have to "catch up on our giving" because we didn't give on a consistent basis.

Some believers say, "I think I'll pray about tithing." That's a bit like praying about whether or not we should read the Bible regularly or whether or not we should be part of a local church. These principles are clear in the Word of God, just like tithing.

I have been asked, "Should we tithe on the net (wages I receive after my taxes are paid) or the gross (wages I receive before the taxes are paid)?" When we pay our taxes to the government, do we pay taxes on the net or on the gross? We pay on whatever we have received (the gross amount). As Christians, we should desire to give everything that we possibly can back to God because of what Jesus Christ has done for us. Remember, tithing is not an option. It is an act of obedience to God. It is a privilege to return to God what is already His.

ATTITUDES TOWARD TITHING

Sometimes Christians believe that tithing is simply an Old Testament doctrine. Dr. Bill Hamon says:

> One divine principle in biblical interpretation is that whatever was established in the Old Testament remains proper as a principle or practice unless the New Testament does away with it. For instance, tithing was established in the Old Testament, but since nothing is stated in the New Testament that abolishes it, then it is still a proper practice for Christians.[4]

Jesus confirms the Old Testament principle of tithing in the New Testament. However, He does not want us to tithe with the attitude of the scribes and Pharisees in Matthew 23:23. The Lord sharply rebuked their attitudes about tithing:

Woe to you, teachers of the law and Pharisees, you hypocrites! You give a tenth of your spices—mint, dill and cummin. But you have neglected the more important matters of the law—justice, mercy and faithfulness. You should have practiced the latter, without neglecting the former.

The religious Pharisees appeared spiritual and godly, but they were not in right standing with God. They tithed right down to the last tiny mint leaf, but their hearts were selfish and hard.

The Lord affirms that we should tithe today, but He is concerned about our attitudes as we give to Him. In the Old Testament, God's people tithed because the law required it. Since the New Testament, we should tithe because the Lord has changed our hearts. It is a privilege to return the tithe back to Him. We tithe as an act of love for our God and also out of a heart of generosity and love for others.

Let's imagine that you ask me to come live in your house. The only stipulation is that, monthly, I need to pay ten percent of all of the things that you provide for me. You fill the refrigerator, put gas in the car, and provide all of my living expenses. It would be ridiculous for me to begin to think that everything is mine. Nothing is mine, because it belongs to you. Giving ten percent reminds me that it all belongs to you. That's what tithing is all about. The Lord's purpose for tithing is to remind us that everything we have belongs to Him.

GOD WILL PROVIDE

When we recognize that everything that we are and have belongs to the Lord, it will be easier for us to trust the Lord to provide for us when we tithe. Even if we do not have much, God will provide when we give to Him. Giving has a way of releasing our finances. Let's learn again from the widow who gave a mite (a fraction of a penny) into the temple treasury. She sacrificially gave more than the many others who threw in large amounts because she gave all that she had.

> *Calling His disciples to Him, Jesus said, "I tell you the truth, this poor widow has put more into the treasury than all the others. They all gave out of their wealth; but she, out of her poverty, put in everything—all she had to live on"* (Mark 12:43-44).

God knows our hearts and honors our obedience in tithing. It might seem like a sacrifice, but in the long run, it helps us to exercise control over our money instead of becoming controlled by it.

What about those who just cannot tithe? For example, if your spouse is unsaved, you may find yourself in a dilemma. He or she may not want you to tithe. If a spouse does not agree to tithe, you cannot give something that is not yours to give. If you are the co-owner of a restaurant, you don't tithe on all the money that you take in because half of it belongs to the other owner. In the same way, you should not give away your family's money against your spouse's wishes.

Here are a few recommendations: appeal to your spouse in faith. For example, you could say, "Could I give some money to the church on a regular basis?" Pray and allow the Holy Spirit to work in his or her heart. Ask the Lord for personal money that you could tithe. Perhaps you occasionally make some extra money at a side job— you could tithe on that personal money. Remember, God looks at our hearts and honors our obedience, no matter how small our tithe may be.

WHERE SHOULD THE TITHE GO?

Where should we give our tithes? As we learned before, Malachi 3:10a says, *"Bring the whole tithe into the storehouse, that there may be food in my house...."*

According to this Scripture, all of the tithes should be placed into the storehouse. The storehouse is where spiritual food is kept to bless those who lead us, feed us, and equip us for ministry. In the Old Testament, the Levites and the priests were responsible to spiritually lead and feed God's people. The tithe paid for the work of those who were set apart for the purpose of ministry to the Lord and to His people. The Levites were dependent upon the faithfulness of God's people in giving tithes to support them: *"I give to the Levites all the tithes in Israel as their inheritance in return for the work they do while serving at the Tent of Meeting"* (Num. 18:21).

Since the Old Testament is a "type and a shadow" of the New Testament, the principle of where to tithe applies in the New Testament as well. We should tithe to the storehouse of our spiritual leaders because they are called by the Lord to minister the Word and encourage us.

Church leaders are called to *"equip the saints for the work of ministry"* (see Eph. 4:11-12 NKJV). They need to be financially supported so that they have enough time to devote to prayer and ministering the Word of God to the saints under their care. In Acts 6:4, the leadership of the early Church knew their responsibility was to single-mindedly *"give* [their] *attention to prayer and the ministry of the word."*

A man once told me, "I give my tithes whenever I see a need." This man did not know it, but he was not giving a tithe, he was giving an offering. An *offering* is anything that we give over and above the ten percent. Tithes are the first ten percent of our income given into the storehouse to provide finances to help support those who are equipping and giving spiritual leadership to the saints in the local church. *"The elders who direct the affairs of the church well are worthy of double honor, especially those whose work is preaching and teaching"* (1 Tim. 5:17). The word *honor* refers to *giving financially* to those who labor among us in spiritual oversight, prayer, teaching, and training in the Word of God.

Now that we know what a tithe is and where it should be given, let's examine the importance of giving both tithes *and* offerings in the next chapter.

ENDNOTES

1. *The Old Testament Hebrew Lexicon*, s.v. "Ma`aser" (tithe), www.studylight.org/lex/heb/view.cgi?number=04643 (accessed 1 Oct 2008).

2. *The Old Testament Hebrew Lexicon*, s.v. "`akal" (devour), www.studylight.org/lex/heb/view.cgi?number=0398 (accessed 1 Oct 2008).

3. *Merriam-Webster's Collegiate Dictionary*, 11th ed., s.v. "Tithe."

4. Dr. Bill Hamon, *Prophets and the Prophetic Movement* (Shippensburg, PA: Destiny Image Publishers, 1990), 197.

THE TITHE
REFLECTION QUESTIONS

1. What does the tithe symbolize?

2. Who will devour our money if we do not tithe?

3. How have you experienced the blessings of God by tithing?

4. Who should be financed from the "storehouse"?

Chapter 15

GIVE BOTH TITHES
AND OFFERINGS

TITHE VS. OFFERING

As we just learned in the last chapter, we need to take care of the needs of those who give us spiritual oversight by giving our tithes. As we give our tithes into the storehouse (the local church where we are fed spiritually), we are taking care of the needs of our spiritual leaders. Galatians 6:6 says that those who are taught God's Word should help provide material support for the instructors: *"Anyone who receives instruction in the word must share all good things with his instructor."*

Verses 7-10 of the same chapter go on to say that if we refuse to give support to these faithful leaders, we are sowing selfishness and reaping destruction. But if we give to these leaders, it is part of *"doing good to all people, especially to those who belong to the family of believers"* (see Gal. 6:10). These faithful leaders in our church are worthy of our support, and we are right in supporting them (see 1 Cor. 9:14; 3 John 6-8; 1 Tim. 5:18).

Our tithe to our local church should be our first priority for giving. This kind of giving is only a place to start, however. We need to give over and beyond our tithes to many worthy causes. "Offerings" are monies given above ten percent. We should give offerings to many places and causes, both within and outside of our local church.

As Christians, we have a responsibility to give to the poor and needy, especially those within the church. We are encouraged to show a concern for the poor. Jesus expected that His people would give generously to the poor. Proverbs 28:27 says, *"He who gives to the poor will lack nothing...."*

In addition, we should also give to those who feed us spiritually from places other than our local church—perhaps through a book, a TV ministry, or another para-church ministry. These are some of the many, many places where we can give our offerings.

I have heard various radio Bible teachers say, "Do not send me your tithes; send me your offerings—that which is over and above ten percent. Your tithe belongs to your local church." I believe those Bible teachers are properly discerning the Scriptures concerning the difference between tithes and offerings.

In conclusion, our tithe should go into the storehouse of the local church, and our offerings should go where we, cheerfully, voluntarily, and generously, believe God is leading us to give.

HEART AND MONEY MATTERS

We usually place our finances in areas that are the most important in our lives. Matthew 6:21 says that wherever we place our money, that's where our hearts will be: *"For where your treasure is, there your heart will be also."*

Riches can demand the total loyalty of one's heart. That's why God tells us that we must decide in our hearts to serve God and not money in Matthew 6:19-24. People who place their money in stocks immediately check out the stock market page whenever they receive their daily newspaper. Why? Because that is where their interests lie; they are concerned about where their finances are placed. Where we give both our tithes and our offerings shows what we place high value on.

Since the Lord has called us to faithfully support our local church, it is important that we are placing our tithes in the storehouse of the local church. We encourage God's people involved in our church to tithe faithfully in obedience to the Lord because, when we tithe to our local church, our hearts are with God's people and with those who serve among us. Consequently, tithing is an issue of the heart—not a law. If we have decided within our hearts to give to our local church and its leadership, we will joyfully give our tithes to the storehouse in our church.

Giving a tithe shows that we trust our leadership. When we are not willing to give a tithe, we begin, even without knowing it, to sow seeds of distrust. Tithing is a test in trust, trust in our God and trust in those whom the Lord has placed in spiritual leadership over our lives.

TITHING—A TEST IN TRUST

Let's take a moment to review. A tithe, as we learned, is ten percent of our income—a reminder that all we have belongs to the Lord. Offerings are gifts that we give to the Lord, His people, and His work that are over and above the ten percent tithe. In the same way that unforgiveness opens the door for the tormenter to bring depression and confusion into people's lives (see Matt. 18:34-35), robbing God of the tithe to the storehouse opens the door for the enemy to rob us. We must trust God and support His work with our tithes, according to Malachi 3:10b: *"'Test me in this,' says the Lord...."*

God is speaking of faith and trust when He tells us to tithe to the storehouse, the place where provisions were kept for the local Levites who were serving God's people. God's people gave to the storehouse in faith because they trusted the Levites to distribute the money properly. Today the same principle of trust applies: the tithe goes into the storehouse of the local church to meet the needs of spiritual leadership who equip and encourage the church. God's plan is for those who spiritually feed and lead us to be supported by tithes:

> *If we have sown spiritual seed among you, is it too much if we reap a material harvest from you? If others have this right of support from you, shouldn't we have it all the more? But we did not use this right. On the contrary, we put up with anything rather than hinder the gospel of Christ. Don't you know that those who work in the temple get their food from the temple, and those who serve at the altar share in what is offered on the altar? In the same way, the Lord has commanded that those who preach the gospel should receive their living from the gospel* (1 Corinthians 9:11-14).

You may wonder, "Where should the pastor (senior leader) of a church tithe?" In some churches, the pastor tithes into the storehouse of those who give him oversight, encouragement, and accountability. This is often a team of spiritual leaders in the pastor's denomination or fellowship of churches.

ARE YOU TITHING?

Malachi 3:8-12 asks the question, "Have you robbed God?" Our response usually is, "Who, me? How could I ever do that?" And then the Lord tells us how—"in tithes and offerings." Are you tithing? If not, according to the Scriptures, you're robbing God. Today is the day to repent before the Lord and to begin to tithe in obedience to the Word of God.

Perhaps you are disobeying the Lord by withholding tithes and offerings because you had a bad experience in the past. A young person, who is the product of a broken home, may not want to get married because of witnessing a bad marriage between his parents while growing up. However, marriage is still a wonderful plan of God. Even though you may have had bad experiences in churches where money was misused, it is still the Lord's plan for us to give our tithes and offerings into the local church. We need to press on, *"...forgetting what is behind and straining toward what is ahead..."* (Phil. 3:13-14).

The Lord will honor you by rebuking the devourer and opening the windows of Heaven. You will also find a new sense of trust in your God and trust in those who serve you in areas of spiritual leadership.

TO THE STOREHOUSE

After God tells His people in Malachi 3 where to tithe—to the storehouse—He promises to pour out a huge blessing if they are obedient: *"...and see if I will not throw open the floodgates of heaven and pour out so much blessing that you will not have room enough for it"* (Mal. 3:10b).

God wants to bless us, but we should tithe where He recommends—the storehouse. Are we tithing, but not to our church family? That would be like buying a hamburger at McDonalds and paying for it at Burger King! In the Old Testament, when the tithe was withheld from the storehouse, the Levites could not fulfill their role. The same is true today. In some parts of the Body of Christ, pastors and other spiritual leaders are struggling financially because the tithes are being withheld in the congregations in which they serve. Consequently, they do not have enough time to effectively serve the people of God because of needing to support themselves through "tent-making" (business). The enemy can devour God's people through disobedience. Of course, some leaders, like Paul the apostle, do choose to make "tents," and this is acceptable and encouraged if the Lord has led them to do so.

What are some examples of giving our tithes to other places besides the storehouse (our church)? Giving our tithes to para-church ministries, missionaries, evangelists, or other ministries are a few examples. Although there are many missionaries, evangelists, and other Christian workers who are reputable men and women of God and need our financial support, according to my understanding of the Scriptures, they should be supported through *offerings*, not through *tithes*. If we give our tithes to them, it can open the door for unbelief and lack of trust to come into our local church family. The tithe should be placed into the storehouse of our local church to be distributed to support those who give us spiritual protection and equip us to minister.

To clarify a common "tithing misunderstanding," the leader of a ministry wrote in his newsletter, "Concerning my statement recently about sending your tithe to our ministry, I received about 35 letters, many from pastors, lovingly reminding me that tithes belong in the local church. I totally agree. I should have clarified my statement. We have quite a number of people on our readers' list who do not attend church, sometimes because their church is shut down or they do not have a suitable church home...Believers really need to find a church home and support it. Until then, however, often my messages are the only spiritual food some people have. Overwhelmingly, those who support this ministry are faithful to support their local church, and they give us over and above their tithes."

Another question to ask is this: are you tithing to the storehouse, but designating your tithe instead of freely giving it like the people in Malachi 3? Some believers are very willing to tithe to the storehouse, but try to control the church by withholding the tithe or a portion of the tithe, or by designating it to be used for certain things only. When we pay our taxes, we do not tell our government to spend some of the taxes on the army and another portion of our taxes to remodel a room or buy new furniture for our president or prime minister. Likewise, in our local church, when we give our tithes to the storehouse, we must trust our spiritual leadership to distribute it in a way that honors the Lord.

EXCUSES TO ROB GOD

There are many reasons why Christians rob God of the tithes and offerings. One reason is simply *ignorance*: *"Truly, these times of ignorance God overlooked, but now commands all men everywhere to repent"* (Acts 17:30 NKJV). If you have been ignorant about this truth, you can repent (turn around) and begin to obey this spiritual truth. We serve a merciful God. He desires to bless us as we obey Him.

Some of God's people do not tithe and give offerings in direct *disobedience to the Word of God*. If we claim to know the Lord, but are not willing to obey His Word, the Scriptures tell us that we are liars. We need to repent and obey the living God: *"The man who says, 'I know Him,' but does not do what He commands is a liar, and the truth is not in him"* (1 John 2:4).

Another reason that some believers do not give tithes and offerings is because of *personal debt*. The Bible says in Galatians 6:7 that

"...a man reaps what he sows." The lack of giving could be part of the reason for being in debt. I read about a Christian businessman who was in debt ten times greater than his yearly income. Yet he obeyed the Lord and began to tithe and give sacrificial offerings. Within the next few years, he saw his entire financial situation turn around. God prospered him, and he became a pastor of a church. The Lord began to use him to teach the truths of the Word of God regarding tithes, offerings, and giving to hundreds of people in his community.

If you find yourself in debt, seek counsel from a trusted Christian who has wisdom in these matters. You may need to develop new habits in sound financial management. Many years ago, a Christian friend showed me how to set up a budget. Managing finances with a budget has been a real blessing to me. A budget will not control our finances, but it will give us a picture of where they are going and what the needs are.

Some people do not give tithes and offerings because they think they are *too poor*. The Lord is not concerned about the amount of money we give; He is more concerned about our attitude toward giving. Even if we have little, we can give in proportion to what God has given us. If we give nothing, we are like a farmer who eats his seed and does not have a crop for the following year. If we eat our seed (using our tithe for something other than what it was intended for), we are hindering the blessing of God in our lives.

This brings us to still another reason why many of God's people withhold their tithes and offerings. They simply *do not trust their leadership*. If we do not trust our leadership in our local church to handle the tithes that we give, then we need to ask the Lord for grace to trust our spiritual leaders. If we still cannot trust them, we may be in the wrong church. First Corinthians 12:18 tells us that God places us in the Body as He wills. It is not the church of *our* choice; it is the church of *His* choice. We need to be among a group of believers where there is a sense of faith and trust in the leadership that God has placed there.

RECEIVE NEW FREEDOM

If you are not tithing and giving offerings, I exhort you to start today by tithing to your church. You will receive a new freedom in your life and relationship with others in the local church family in which you serve. In addition, ask God to bless you so that you can give generous offerings to ministries of integrity. There are many ministries that are worthy of our gifts and offerings; however, be sure to check out where you give. The Lord holds us responsible to give offerings to reputable ministries. Do not be afraid to do your homework before giving.

Remember, tithing is a test in trust—a trust in our God who has promised to rebuke the devourer and open the windows of Heaven. And it is also a trust in the spiritual leaders in our local church as we tithe into the storehouse. The Lord desires to set us free to give our tithes and offerings to Him joyfully. And He desires to bless us as His children who obey His voice. John 8:36 tells us, *"So if the Son sets you free, you will be free indeed."*

May the Lord bless you and open the windows of Heaven for you as you walk in obedience to these spiritual truths. In the next chapter of this book, we will look at how to manage the money and material wealth with which the Lord has blessed us.

GIVE BOTH TITHES AND OFFERINGS
REFLECTION QUESTIONS

1. In your own words, explain the difference between a tithe and an offering.

2. How is trust a part of giving your tithe?

3. What is wrong with designating where we want our tithe to go within the local church?

4. Describe ways that you have been set free to give—in both your tithes and offerings.

Chapter 16

MANAGING YOUR GOD-GIVEN FINANCES

FAITHFUL WITH WHAT WE HAVE

The finances and possessions that the Lord has given to us belong to Him. We are simply managers of that which He has given. First Corinthians 4:2 says, *"Now it is required that those who have been given a trust must prove faithful."*

We are entrusted with God's money. So then, the finances and possessions that we have should be used to honor God and build His Kingdom. We must faithfully use what God has given us.

The Lord also wants us to be content with the finances that He's given to us. Paul said, *"…I have learned to be content whatever the circumstances"* (Phil. 4:11).

To be content is to be free from complaining. There have been times when our family has lived with very little and other times when we have been abundantly blessed. Either way, God has called us to be content and to triumphantly live above our changing circumstances.

People today often want their needs gratified immediately, so they go deeply into debt to buy the things that they think they cannot do without. This is a financial mistake and breeds discontent.

It is also a mistake to want to get rich quick instead of paying the price faithfully, obeying God, day by day. This kind of "lottery thinking" or "waiting until I get a big break" is really "poverty thinking." If we focus on a distant chance that may come, we will be hindered from moving forward financially today. Financial advancement comes to those who apply God's principles on a consistent, long-term basis (see Heb. 6:12).

Remember the parable of the talents (see Matt. 25:14-30)? One man had five talents and was faithful with the five. Another man had two. The Lord knew he was responsible enough to handle two talents. The third man only received one. Why did God give him just one talent? That was all he could handle at that point. God knows what we can handle. When we are faithful with what He has given, He blesses us with more.

PROVIDE FOR OUR FAMILIES

The Lord wants to bless us financially in order to meet the needs of our family:

If anyone does not provide for his relatives, and especially for his immediate family, he has denied the faith and is worse than an unbeliever (1 Timothy 5:8).

For even when we were with you, we gave you this rule: "If a man will not work, he shall not eat" (2 Thessalonians 3:10).

A man gave his life to the Lord and was convinced that he should spend all of his time witnessing. He spent his time out on the beach, witnessing every day, while his family was nearly starving. He believed that somehow God would be obligated to provide for his family since he was so busy doing "God's work." When his Christian friends challenged him to take care of his family, he became defensive. "Wasn't he telling others about Jesus? What could be more important than that?" The truth was that he was disobeying the Word of God. God was not telling him to be out witnessing when his family was not being properly taken care of. If the Lord calls you as a missionary who "lives by faith," it is important to not do it at the expense of your family. I have been privileged to proclaim the Gospel and train Christian leaders in various parts of the world. However, my first responsibility is for my own family. Any Christian who refuses to provide for his own family has denied the faith and is worse than an unbeliever.

Some people say to me, "I want to be involved in a full-time ministry, supported by the church." This can be a noble desire; however, the truth is that everyone is involved in a full-time ministry. Every working Christian is in full-time ministry, no matter what their job. We are called to minister at our workplaces.

So why do we work? Is it to have money to buy expensive material possessions? Not at all. The Bible tells us that we work to give to him who is in need (see Eph. 4:28). It starts with providing for our own families and helping those whom the Lord has placed around us.

It is a blessing to be able to work. Don't wait for the perfect job. Start somewhere, and God will give you the perfect job in the future as you are faithful in the opportunity that He has given you today.

INVESTING OUR MASTER'S WEALTH

How do we invest our Master's wealth to see His Kingdom built in a way that will honor Him the most? First of all, we invest the

Lord's money to evangelize the world. Remember the story of the prodigal son? His father gave half of his wealth to the son who promptly wasted it. That young man eventually came back to his father, but it cost his father half of his fortune. In other words, the father used all of that money to see one soul saved. The Bible tells us in Mark 8:36-37 that we cannot put a price-tag on a soul: *"What good is it for a man to gain the whole world, yet forfeit his soul? Or what can a man give in exchange for his soul?"*

In our church, we encourage every Christian to support a missionary somewhere in the world. Why? According to the Bible, wherever we place our money, that is where our heart will be (see Matt. 6:21). And since God loves the world so much, our missionary support keeps our hearts at the same place as our God's—reaching the world. The money that we give to support a missionary of our choice is not taken from our tithe. It is taken from the 90 percent—an offering. Anything that is given above the ten percent is an offering to the Lord. By investing our offerings into someone like a missionary, we are helping to invest the Lord's money to evangelize the world.

A practical way to invest our wealth is to invest in stocks or bonds or mutual funds that give a financial increase. Like the man in the Parable of the Talents who invested wisely, we will receive an increase with wise investments. This increase can help expand the Kingdom of God.

MONEY AND RELATIONSHIPS

We can also use the Lord's money to honor Him and build His Kingdom by using it to build relationships. Jesus told the story of a manager who was being fired. His boss said, "Clean up your accounts; you're going to be fired." So the manager quickly found a man who owed the boss eight hundred gallons of oil. He said to the man, "Pay me for four hundred gallons." He found someone else who owed a thousand bushels of wheat and said, "Just rip up the original bill and pay for eight hundred bushels." The boss of the corporation came back and saw what the manager had done. Instead of being angry, the Bible says in Luke 16:8-9,

> *The master commended the dishonest manager because he had acted shrewdly. For the people of this world are more shrewd in dealing with their own kind than are the people of the light. I tell you, use worldly wealth to gain friends for yourselves, so that when it is gone, you will be welcomed into eternal dwellings.*

The manager was commended by his master because he was acting very shrewdly. He used his master's finances to build relationships. He knew that he was going to be without a job and that he needed relationships with other people. Although this manager was dishonest, and Jesus never condones dishonesty, there is a truth that we can learn from this story. Jesus says that the people in the world are shrewder than God's children. In other words, many non-Christians have learned to use finances to build relationships, while in the Church, we have often not understood this important principle.

We need to use our finances to build relationships. Take someone out for a meal, and you will be building a relationship that will last for eternity. A young man once told me that, as a little boy, he met an older Christian man who bought him an ice cream cone. That 35 cent ice cream cone opened him up to God through his relationship with this Christian man. Do you know why? The man was using his money to build relationships.

Baking a cake for your neighbor will help to build a relationship. Inviting someone into your home for hospitality or for a meal is using the money that the Lord has entrusted to you to build relationships with people that will last for eternity. The Bible says in Matthew 5:16, *"...Let your light shine before men, that they may see your good deeds and praise your Father in heaven."*

Our actions speak louder than our words. The way we use our money can cause people in the world around us to fall in love with Jesus Christ and live eternally with Him. Remember, Jesus Christ lives in us (see Gal. 2:20). People often learn to trust Jesus as they learn to trust us.

HELPING THE POOR

In both the New and the Old Testament, the Lord requires us to give to help those who are poor. James 1:27 says, *"Religion that God our Father accepts as pure and faultless is this: to look after orphans and widows in their distress and to keep oneself from being polluted by the world."*

Deuteronomy 15:7-8 tells us, *"If there is a poor man among your brothers...do not be hardhearted or tightfisted toward your poor brother. Rather be openhanded and freely lend him whatever he needs."*

Jesus said:

For I was hungry and you gave me something to eat, I was thirsty and you gave me something to drink, I was a stranger and you invited me in, I needed clothes and you clothed me, I was sick and you looked after me, I was in prison and you came to visit me (Matthew 25:35-36).

And then He said, a few verses later, *"...whatever you did for one of the least of these brothers of mine, you did for me"* (Matt. 25:40). In other words, when we help someone who is hurting because we love Jesus Christ, we are doing it unto Jesus.

I believe we will stand before God, and He will say, "Remember the time you invited Me into your home?" or "Remember the time you helped Me when I was struggling financially?" Every time we invite someone into our home or help someone because of Jesus, we are doing it to Him.

If the Lord has blessed us financially, it is for the purpose of blessing those around us: *"He who has pity on the poor lends to the Lord, and He will pay back what he has given"* (Prov. 19:17 NKJV).

According to the Bible, when we give to someone who is poor, we are placing the money in God's bank—the greatest bank in the whole world. If God tells you to give someone a certain amount of money, you are literally investing that money in the Lord's bank. The Lord will pay you back with His blessing when you invest money in His bank by giving to those who are poor.

MEETING NEEDS IN THE KINGDOM

The Lord also wants to bless us so that we can meet needs in the Body of Christ. Second Corinthians 8:14 tells us, *"At the present time your plenty will supply what they need, so that in turn their plenty will supply what you need. Then there will be equality."*

BUILDING YOUR LIFE *on the* BASIC TRUTHS *of* CHRISTIANITY

In other words, when one person has an abundance, he will supply the lack that someone else has. It reminds me of a balance scale.
If my side of the scale is too heavy, I take some of the weight off my
side and place it on your side of the scale. If you have extra, you give
to someone else so that they can be blessed by your abundance. If
they have extra finances and you are going through a financial struggle, they can give to you so that you also may have what you need.

There are enough resources in the Body of Christ to meet every
need. I am not talking about a type of communism. Communism
coerces people and forces "equality" on people under its influence.
People should never be forced to give. In the Kingdom of God, the
Holy Spirit gives the Lord's people a desire to give to serve those
who have a need in the Body of Christ, both in our communities and
in the mission field.

As we give, the Lord wants us to have proper attitudes and
motives. Second Corinthians 9:7 gives us a few biblical attitudes to
consider as we give: *"Each man should give what he has decided in
his heart to give, not reluctantly or under compulsion, for God loves
a cheerful giver."*

First of all, let's give cheerfully. I know of one church in the state
of Texas where the people are so excited about giving that they cheer
and clap every time there is an offering given.

God has called us to give freely and willingly. Matthew 10:8b
says, *"...Freely you have received, freely give."* We also should not
give grudgingly or because we have to. We need to give because we
want to.

You may ask, "How much should I give"? When we go to a
meeting of believers at our local church and they take a special offering, the Lord will give us a sense of peace so that we can know how

much we should give. The more we grow in the Lord and give, the more we grow in faith. Again, we don't give grudgingly or because we have to, but we give because it is a joy to give back to God that which is His already.

GIVE AND IT WILL BE GIVEN

A friend of mine, a new Christian, was serving in the military. One day his friend borrowed money from him and did not pay him back. My friend struggled with unforgiveness, until he read this Scripture in Luke 6:33-35:

> *And if you do good to those who are good to you, what credit is that to you? Even "sinners" do that. And if you lend to those from whom you expect repayment, what credit is that to you? Even "sinners" lend to "sinners," expecting to be repaid in full. But love your enemies, do good to them, and lend to them without expecting to get anything back. Then your reward will be great, and you will be sons of the Most High, because He is kind to the ungrateful and wicked.*

When we give or lend money to others, it must be in faith. Whether or not it is returned to us, we must strive to keep our attitudes pure and continue to love even our "enemies."

God has called us to give in faith. Luke 6:38 says, *"Give, and it will be given to you. A good measure, pressed down, shaken together and running over, will be poured into your lap. For with the measure you use, it will be measured to you."*

As we give, God says that He wants to bless us by giving back to us the same measure that we give to others. He is the One who is responsible to bless us. Although our motivation for giving must always be out of our love for God, the Lord desires to bless us when we give in obedience to Him. Many do not receive God's financial blessings because they have not exercised their faith and do not expect to receive God's abundance.

God also calls us to give liberally. Second Corinthians 9:6 says, *"Remember this: Whoever sows sparingly will also reap sparingly, and whoever sows generously will also reap generously."*

Let's give to others just as Jesus has been so faithful to give to us. It is, however, important to check out where we give. A pastor friend confided in me that his church had given thousands of dollars to a man in another nation only to find out that this man was embezzling money from the church for his own personal use. Of course they stopped giving to the man. We need to be sure that we are giving to reputable Christian ministries. It is often good to give to those with whom we have a close personal relationship. We can trust them because we know them and see genuine spiritual fruit in their lives.

And finally, the Lord's desire is that we prosper. Second Corinthians 8:9 says, *"For you know the grace of our Lord Jesus Christ, that though He was rich, yet for your sakes He became poor, so that you through His poverty might become rich."*

Jesus Christ took the curse of poverty for us. He wants us to be blessed spiritually, relationally, physically, mentally, and financially. But remember, when He blesses us, He takes a risk. We may choose to trust in our financial riches instead of trusting in the living God. He desires to bless us so that we can bless those around us. May the Lord bless you as you fulfill your responsibility as a good manager (steward) of the finances that He has entrusted to you.

MANAGING YOUR GOD-GIVEN FINANCES
REFLECTION QUESTIONS

1. What does First Timothy 5:8 teach us about taking care of our families? Examine your life; are you motivated to work for the right reasons?

2. In what ways are you investing your wealth for the Kingdom of God?

3. Repeat Matthew 5:16 aloud while changing the word *your* to *my*. Make it your prayer.

4. What is the difference between God's equality and communism's way?

PART V

Called to Minister

Chapter 17

EVERYONE CAN MINISTER

WE ARE EQUIPPED TO MINISTER

Recently a soccer enthusiast told me of his experience at one of the World Cup soccer games. He paid $150 for a seat and joined thousands of fans who watched 22 talented players kick a ball around on a soccer field. Although he loved soccer, he was not allowed to play—he was a spectator only. His story reminded me of the Church today. Think about it. A group of "spectator" Christians gathers together each Sunday morning to watch as the pastor performs his duties. Is this what the Lord desires for His Church? I do not believe so. Every believer can be a minister.

Pastors or other Church leaders are in place to help or equip every believer to minister. The Bible tells us in Ephesians 4:11-12 that the Lord releases spiritual leaders with specific gifts for two basic purposes: *"And He Himself gave some to be apostles, some prophets, some evangelists, and some pastors and teachers, for the equipping of the saints for the work of ministry, for the edifying of the body of Christ"* (NKJV).

According to this Scripture, these spiritual leaders with particular gifts are given to *"equip the saints to do the work of ministry"* and to *"build up [edify] the body of Christ."* Christ gives these leaders specific leadership gifts so that they can prepare God's people for works of service and so that the Body of Christ can grow as God intended. When these leaders train and equip every saint to minister, the Church grows. If every believer does not learn how to serve others, God's Church becomes paralyzed: only part of the Body is being used.

If most of your body parts shut down, you would be suffering from a partial paralysis. Much of the Church of Jesus Christ today has become paralyzed because the important truth of all of the saints doing the work of ministry is overlooked. God is restoring a basic truth to His Church which involves the dynamic of every believer being called as a minister.

The leadership of the early Church, including apostles, prophets, evangelists, pastors, and teachers, realized that their focus needed to be on prayer and ministering the Word of God: *"We will...give our attention to prayer and the ministry of the word"* (Acts 6:3b-4).

Before they could give themselves continually to prayer and the ministry of the Word, the leaders had to train each believer to minister. Only then could they be free from needing to do everything themselves. As they obeyed this spiritual principle, thousands came into the Kingdom of God, and the Church grew rapidly during the first century.

EVERYONE CAN SERVE

Since the Scriptures tell us that the saints are called to do the work of ministry, let's look again at who the saints really are. The truth is this: if you are a Christian, born again by the Spirit of God, you are a saint. We do not become saints when we get to Heaven. We are saints right now. When you look in the mirror in the morning, I encourage you to say, "I am a saint." The Bible says that the saints are the ones who are called to do the work of ministry (see Eph. 4:12). Thousands of believers today are unfulfilled because they are not fulfilling the purpose that God intended for them—to minister to others.

What does the word *ministry* or *minister* really mean? Webster's dictionary says, "to minister means to serve, to wait, or to attend."[1] If you go to a restaurant, the waiter or waitress is ministering to you. They serve you or wait on you at your table. That is a type of ministry. If you go to a hospital, you will see hospital attendants who are waiting on, serving, or ministering to the patients. The terms *serve* and *minister* can be used interchangeably.

Every Christian is called by God to minister to other people. It is a privilege to minister to and serve others. There are many different ways to minister and many different types of ministry; however, each person is called to serve others in the name of Jesus. The Bible says in Mark 16:17-18 that some signs will accompany true disciples and confirm that the Gospel message is genuine:

> *And these signs will accompany those who believe: In My name they will drive out demons; they will speak in new tongues; they will pick up snakes with their hands; and when they drink deadly poison, it will not hurt them at all; they will place their hands on sick people, and they will get well.*

This Scripture speaks of various kinds of ministry to which the Lord calls His people today. It does not say that these signs shall follow pastors or apostles or evangelists. It says *"these signs will accompany those who believe."* Every Christian who truly believes in Jesus is called of God to be a minister to others with power and authority.

ARE WE EXERCISING SPIRITUALLY?

In today's Church, we often have a warped understanding of what it means to minister. But God is beginning to train and teach us to have a proper understanding of ministry from His perspective.

In the past, we have often thought that the pastor of the local church is responsible for all of the ministry—that the ministry is accomplished only by the clergy, the trained, or the supported. Because of this attitude, many believers in the Church today are very weak spiritually, and understandably so. If you and I never exercised, we would become physically weak. In the same way, if we do not exercise spiritually, we become weak spiritually: *"But solid food is for the mature, who by constant use have trained themselves to distinguish good from evil"* (Heb. 5:14).

We become spiritually mature by practicing and experiencing what God has told us to do. God has called every believer to be a minister for Him. We can be only a few days old in the Lord and already begin to minister to others by telling them what Jesus Christ has done for us.

When the pastor does all of the spiritual exercise, he burns himself out. The saints in the church are not exercising spiritually and remain weak, causing the entire church to be weak. Imagine a pastor doing 4,000 push-ups every day! In a spiritual sense, that is what has happened in the Church today.

I firmly believe that the Lord has called pastors and other spiritual leaders to train the saints so that every believer can be involved in ministry and maturing in Christ. When God's people are not exercising, they are no longer growing. Since God has given each of us different gifts and abilities, we all need to use these gifts to minister.

As each believer is fulfilling what the Lord has called him or her to do, a wonderful thing happens. God begins to build His Church through His people from house to house and in each community. Ministry does not just happen in our church services; it happens at our schools, our places of work, and in our homes as we reach out to others. All, then, are fulfilled because they are using the gifts that God has given them. This is the Lord's plan for building His Church.

HOW TO MINISTER

There are various ways to minister. For example, washing someone's car or giving them a ride to work is a type of ministry. Others may be gifted to bake a cake, giving it to someone as a "labor of love." Encouraging others, praying for the sick, and serving children in a children's ministry or Sunday school are all types of ministry. Many times, people think that *to minister* means *to teach or preach.* But that is only one of hundreds of ways that we can minister in the name of Jesus.

When Jesus walked on the earth, He could be at only one place at one time. God the Father's strategy was for Jesus to go to the cross, then be raised from the dead, ascend into Heaven, and later send the Holy Spirit to His people. The Holy Spirit then would indwell the Lord's people. Now, rather than only Jesus walking the earth offering hope to people, there would be thousands of believers filled with the same Holy Spirit, ministering in Jesus' name throughout the world.

217

We have received the Holy Spirit and are called by the Lord to be ministers. Everywhere Jesus went, He ministered to people. Everywhere we go, God has called us to minister to others—in our homes, communities, schools, and jobs, and we can do it only by His strength:

> Not *that we are competent in ourselves to claim anything for ourselves, but our competence comes from God. He has made us competent as ministers of a new covenant—not of the letter but of the Spirit; for the letter kills, but the Spirit gives life* (2 Corinthians 3:5-6).

I will never forget the first time I ever taught at a Bible study as a young man. I was scared because this was something new for me. I also realized that God's strength in me would pull me through. My competence was from God.

Many years ago, I served as a worship leader. The first time that I ever led God's people in worship was in a church meeting where there were no musical instruments. I was given a small, round pitch pipe to get the proper key for the song. The first time, I blew the pitch pipe exceptionally loud and was extremely embarrassed! I looked for a hole in the floor to fall through, especially when I noticed that some of the people were giggling at my expense. It was a humbling experience, but by the grace of God, I got through that first song. As I continued to practice, realizing that I was called by God to minister in this way, I began to enjoy leading others in worshiping our Lord.

OUT OF THE COMFORT ZONE

Each of us has an area in our lives that is comfortable, that we sometimes call our "comfort zone." We often find it hard to move out of our comfort zone into new things, but God has called us to take steps of faith. When Peter walked on the water, he moved far beyond his comfort zone (see Matt. 14:30)!

God has called us to be people of faith and to depend on the ability of God within us to help us accomplish His work. The Bible says, *"...Without faith it is impossible to please God..."* (Heb. 11:6). Ministry to others will often require us to move beyond our comfort zone.

Our homes are excellent places of ministry. Jesus spent much of His time in the homes of people. The Book of Acts is filled with examples of people meeting in homes: fellowshipping together, learning together, and ministering to one another. Invite people into your home—for a meal or to spend time in fellowship. Exciting things can happen when people sit down together to eat a meal, play a game, or just talk and laugh together. People can relax when we meet them on their own level and let them know that we, too, are real people with real problems. We can ask the Lord for an opportunity to pray with them, and it can be a life-changing experience. Keep in mind that you are a saint who is called to minister.

The Lord may want to use you to give someone godly counsel. You may feel that, since you're not a professional counselor, God can't use you, but the Bible says in Isaiah 9:6, *"...He will be called...Wonderful Counselor."* Jesus is the Counselor, and He lives within us. When people need solutions to problems in their lives, and I don't know the answers, I know that Jesus, the Counselor, lives in me. He has the answers. I pray and ask the Lord to speak to them and tell them what to do. Sometimes I can steer them toward other Christians who may be able to answer their questions.

Remember, the Lord has given you a powerful testimony. As you share your testimony with others, you'll find that the Holy Spirit will use you to speak the truth and that others will be built up in faith. Perhaps you are afraid that someone will ask you a question that you don't have the answer to. If you are unsure of the correct answers, it is appropriate to say, "I don't know, but perhaps I can ask someone who does know." None of us have all of the answers. That's why the Lord placed different gifts in different people in His Church. We need one another.

HIS ABILITY, NOT OURS

The Lord wants us to be available for Him to use us to minister to others in many different ways. When our new church first started, one Sunday morning I was responsible to preach, and the next Sunday morning I was responsible to minister to the children. Ministering to the children helped prepare me for other types of ministry that the Lord would call me to in future years.

Regardless of the ministry to which the Lord has called you, you do not minister by your own ability but by His ability that is within you. If you serve in a nursery, you can pray, laying your hands on these special children, ministering to them in Jesus' name. God has called each of us as Christians to minister wherever we go, asking the Lord to open our eyes so that we can see people as He sees them. John 3:16 tells us, *"God so loved the world that He gave His only begotten Son, that whoever believes in Him should not perish but have everlasting life."* God loves people, and He lives in us! He has called us to encourage and serve the people around us.

Service is often done in practical ways. The Lord may call you to minister by helping a neighbor change a flat tire in the rain. God will be repairing a car through you! Sometimes serving requires us to do what the Lord has called us to do rather than what we *feel* like doing. If we have been truly crucified with Christ, the Bible tells us that we are dead to doing what we want to do: *"I have been cruci-fied with Christ and I no longer live, but Christ lives in me. The life I live in the body, I live by faith in the Son of God, who loved me and gave Himself for me"* (Gal. 2:20).

The old you is dead, and Jesus Christ now lives inside of you. He has called you to be a minister for Him.

LOVE CONQUERS ALL

I was speaking to a professional counselor who had years of psy-chological training. "You know," he said, "some people think that in order to help others they need to have all kinds of training." Then he went on to say, "I find that what people really need is just to have someone to love them." This counselor was not minimizing the need for training; however, he was talking about meeting the deeper need that is in the hearts of men and women today—the need to be loved.

That is what ministry is really all about. Jesus has called us to love people. We love people by listening to them and genuinely car-ing about the needs they have. We should not feel fearful or inade-quate to minister to others. The Bible says, *"...Perfect love drives out fear..."* (1 John 4:18).

When I realize that God loves me and that He loves the person to whom I am ministering, His perfect love will cast out the fear. The more we spend time with Jesus, the more Christ will be able to min-ister through us. As we spend time with Jesus, those around us will perceive that we have the ability to minister to them because His love and boldness will be evident in our lives just as it was with Peter and John: *"When they saw the courage of Peter and John and realized that they were unschooled, ordinary men, they were astonished and they took note that these men had been with Jesus"* (Acts 4:13).

When we feel weak, it is then that we can be truly strong because we know that God's grace is sufficient for us. Paul pleaded with the Lord to take away a "thorn in the flesh." But the Lord told him that His strength would be made perfect through Paul's weakness, according to Second Corinthians 12:9-10:

But He said to me, "My grace is sufficient for you, for My power is made perfect in weakness." Therefore I will boast all the more gladly about my weaknesses, so that Christ's power may rest on me. That is why, for Christ's sake, I delight in weaknesses, in insults, in hardships, in persecutions, in difficulties. For when I am weak, then I am strong.

God's grace is always sufficient to enable us to live our daily lives. When we draw near to Christ, He will help us in every situation, giving us strength and comfort. We can minister to others by faith, through the strength of Jesus Christ.

ENDNOTE

1. Noah Webster, *American Dictionary of the English Language* (1828), s.v. "Minister."

EVERYONE CAN MINISTER
REFLECTION QUESTIONS

1. What is the role of spiritual leaders in the Church, according to Ephesians 4:11-12? How do these leaders train us to minister?

2. Are any of the signs of Mark 16:17-18 happening in your life?

3. List several things that you are able to do for others.

4. Describe some situations when you moved out of your comfort zone.

Chapter 18

WE ARE CALLED
TO SERVE

IF YOU WANT TO BE GREAT

One day the mother of James and John came to Jesus with a special request:

> *Then the mother of Zebedee's sons came to Jesus with her sons and, kneeling down, asked a favor of Him.... "Grant that one of these two sons of mine may sit at your right and the other at your left in your kingdom"* (Matthew 20:20-21).

The Bible tells us that the other disciples were indignant. They couldn't believe that James and John had the audacity to expect to sit on the right and left hand of Jesus in His Kingdom. They, of course, were still thinking that Jesus was going to set up an earthly kingdom. The 12 disciples had a wrong understanding of ministry and leadership entirely. Jesus tried to correct this wrong thinking when He told His disciples:

> *...You know that the rulers of the Gentiles lord it over them, and their high officials exercise authority over them. Not so with you. Instead, whoever wants to become great among you must be your servant, and whoever wants to be first must*

be your slave—just as the Son of Man did not come to be served, but to serve, and to give His life as a ransom for many (Matthew 20:25-28).

Jesus told His disciples that those who are under the world's system do not understand the principle of ministry and servanthood. Someone who is a leader in the world is often a person who exercises his power and control over people. But Jesus advocated a new way. He said that true leadership exemplifies servanthood. Servanthood is characterized through serving. Jesus Christ, the King of the universe, came to this earth to be a servant. Every chance that He got, He served people and set an example for us. We also are called to be ministers (servants) to others in His name. We must minister to and help others—this is a true measure of greatness.

SERVING EQUALS MINISTRY

What, then, does it really mean to serve? As was mentioned earlier, the words *serving* and *ministry* are really synonymous. James and John wanted to be great in the Kingdom. They thought greatness came from having the right position, but Jesus said that greatness came through serving. Greatness does not depend on our talents or our abilities, but on our willingness to serve.

A servant is simply a person who is devoted to another. I love to watch people. And as I travel throughout the world, I've found an amazing truth. Wherever I find a truly "great man or woman of God," I notice that he or she has the heart of a servant.

Years ago, as a young pastor, I was at a leadership meeting in Dayton, Ohio. I found myself watching an elderly man, a leader in the Body of Christ, who has now gone on to be with the Lord.

Everywhere he went, he served others. I watched him as he reached out to a bell boy in the hotel, telling him about Jesus Christ. I watched him as he responded in gentleness and compassion to those who came and asked him questions about spiritual things. He was truly a servant.

The mark of greatness in the Kingdom of God is our willingness and obedience to serve others. One day, Jesus told a parable to a group of guests who were invited into the house of a ruler of the Pharisees:

When someone invites you to a wedding feast, do not take the place of honor, for a person more distinguished than you may have been invited. If so, the host who invited both of you will come and say to you, "Give this man your seat." Then, humiliated, you will have to take the least important place. But when you are invited, take the lowest place, so that when your host comes, he will say to you, "Friend, move up to a better place." Then you will be honored in the presence of all your fellow guests. For everyone who exalts himself will be humbled, and he who humbles himself will be exalted (Luke 14:8-11).

The Lord warns us that we should never exalt ourselves or try to take the best places. Instead, we need to be willing to serve in the background. D.L. Moody, the great evangelist who was used of God to see more than one million souls come into God's Kingdom, always liked to sit in the background. He was a servant. If we honor the Lord with humility and servanthood, in due time we will be exalted.

SERVING IN LOVE

A friend of mine serves as a Christian leader in our nation. Years ago, when he was a young Christian, he moved to a major city. He has a charismatic personality and had studied the Bible. He was enthusiastic and excited to teach others. One evening he went to a Bible study and offered to teach the Word at future meetings. The group leader told him that he appreciated my friend's willingness; however, he really needed someone to set up the chairs. So week after week, my friend could be found setting up the chairs for the meeting. He was willing to be a servant, and today he is a noted leader in the Body of Christ, teaching the Bible throughout the world.

The Scriptures tell us in First Corinthians 8:1, *"...Knowledge puffs up, but love builds up."* Too much knowledge can make us arrogant, but love will always build others up. I have met people who thought that to be involved in ministry meant that they were called to preach or teach rather than to serve the people of God. Preaching and teaching are valid ministries that are needed in the Church today. However, all ministry, including the ministry of preaching and teaching, must come from a heart of love and compassion. Preachers and teachers who are called by God have a desire to serve those whom they teach. Only love will build people up. Too much knowledge, including knowledge of the Bible, without a heart of love and compassion, can cause us to be puffed up with pride.

Many times God's people need to minister in menial and practical ways before the Lord will release them into a ministry of preaching and teaching. Those who are willing to serve in these humble beginnings often are being prepared by the Lord to minister in greater ways because they have developed a servant's heart.

Regardless of how much training or knowledge a person may have, the Lord is looking for those who are willing to serve. If we are willing to serve, He can truly make us great. If we are not willing to serve, regardless of our training or background, we cannot be great in the Kingdom.

HOW CAN I SERVE YOU?

Why didn't Jesus take you and me to Heaven as soon as we were born again? I believe the answer is: so that we can serve here on the earth and help many people come into His Kingdom through a relationship with Jesus Christ. Consequently, the bottom line is this: every believer is called to serve. We are called to serve our families, people at our place of employment, people to whom we are committed in our small groups, and other believers in our local church. The question we should ask ourselves wherever we go is, "How can I serve today?"

Maybe in your church you could serve by participating in a drama or puppet ministry as you minister to children. You may be called to minister to prisoners. Some may serve by picking up litter in a neighborhood. Perhaps you could visit the elderly and pray for them or serve meals to those going through a stressful time in their lives. Providing transportation for someone in a time of need can be a tremendous act of service.

You are a true minister when you serve others. Jesus never said, "I am the king, come worship me." He simply served. James 4:10 says, *"Humble yourselves before the Lord, and He will lift you up."*

Some time back, a pastor who had served the Lord faithfully for many years became a member of our church. One of the first questions that he asked when he came was, "How can I serve?" He was not thinking, "When can I preach a sermon?" He understood the importance of true ministry, serving in the Body of Christ. It is the people with the attitude of a servant who the Lord will use to build His Church in a powerful way.

I have found that I am drawn to others who are willing to serve. As Jesus went about serving others, people were attracted to Him. When we have the heart of a servant, the Lord will cause people to be drawn to us so that we can pray for them and minister to them. As we reach out beyond ourselves to serve others, people will be drawn into the Kingdom of God. People usually do not come to Jesus because we have a lot of Bible knowledge, even though it is important to understand the Scriptures. People are attracted to Christ when they see the heart of a servant exemplified through our lives.

TOUCHING OTHERS BY SERVING

According to the Bible, people around us will glorify our God in Heaven because of the way that they see us serve. Jesus said, "...*Let your light shine before men, that they may see your good deeds and praise your Father in heaven*" (Matt. 5:16).

A family I know made a commitment one winter to keep two elderly neighbors' sidewalks clean after it snowed. They shoveled cheerfully, even though they got an extraordinary amount of snow that winter!

I served as a pastor for many years. Because of the many people who came to our church, I was not able to meet everyone who came to our Sunday services. There were simply too many people. But do you know who they met? They met the people who parked the cars, those who greeted them at the door, those who ushered them to their seats, those who invited them to a small group meeting in their home, and those who served their children in the children's ministry. They experienced Jesus in these precious saints who were ministering to them and their children. By this, they were drawn into the Kingdom of God.

You see, it is Jesus working through each of us that makes all the difference in the world. As the people in our church touched those around them with the love of Jesus Christ, hundreds of precious people became part of God's Kingdom and became committed to our local church. Jesus used hundreds of ministers, through practical service, to minister to those whom God drew into His Kingdom.

Everywhere I go, I find people in the Church who have a servant's heart. One time in Africa, I was blessed by a businessman who was constantly finding opportunities to serve. He was not looking for a position in the church, but his desire was to be supported by his business so that he could better serve Jesus and the people of God in his local church. He was truly a minister.

Although the Lord does call specific people to be supported by the local church so that they can equip others to minister, let us never forget that *every* saint is called to be a minister.

THE MINISTRY OF "HELPS"

Jesus spent His time training and encouraging His 12 disciples; He modeled for them what the Kingdom of God was all about. These disciples also served Jesus in a ministry of *helps* similar to what we see in First Corinthians 12:28: "*...God has appointed these in the church: first apostles, second prophets, third teachers, after that miracles, then gifts of healing, **helps**, administrations, varieties of tongues*" (NKJV).

The ministry of *helps* is a ministry of giving aid, assistance, support, or relief to another person involved in ministry. It is giving practical assistance to someone so that he can fulfill his responsibilities to God. Jesus' disciples helped Him fulfill the ministry that His Father had given to Him. A group of women also aided Jesus in His ministry, serving Him in many ways so that He had time to pray, preach, and minister healing to the people around Him (see Luke 8:1-3).

One day, Jesus sent His disciples into Jerusalem to find a colt, untie it, and bring it back to Him so that He could ride it to Jerusalem (see Matt. 21:1-11). Another time, the disciples prepared the upper room for the Last Supper (Matt. 26:17-30). They were serving in the ministry of helps.

Yet another time, thousands of people were gathered together to hear Jesus teach. It was getting late, and the people were hungry. When Jesus asked what was available to eat, they discovered that they had only five loaves of bread and two fish. Jesus prayed over the loaves and fish; it supernaturally multiplied—in fact, 12 basketfuls were left over after all of the people were fed (see Matt. 14:13-21). The disciples were involved in the ministry of helps as they distributed the food to the hungry people. I personally believe that there was one leftover basketful of food for each disciple who had served.

Another time, Jesus realized that He needed to pay the temple tax, so He sent Peter to catch a fish. When the fish was caught, a coin was found to pay the taxes (see Matt. 17:27). Peter was serving in the ministry of helps when he caught the fish and paid the taxes.

I am constantly looking for future spiritual leaders. The leaders God is looking for are those who are willing to serve in the ministry of helps as God prepares them for future leadership.

TRAINING FOR FUTURE MINISTRY

Jesus' disciples learned faithfulness by serving practically. If we are faithful in small things, God knows that He can trust us with greater responsibilities: *"He who is faithful in what is least is faithful also in much; and he who is unjust in what is least is unjust also in much"* (Luke 16:10 NKJV).

Moses was trained to be a leader by serving. Before he delivered the children of Israel out of Egypt, God placed him in the ministry of helps—serving his father-in-law by tending sheep in the desert for 40 years.

Later on, Joshua served Moses in a ministry of helps capacity while he was being trained to take over Moses' responsibility of leadership for the children of Israel. Many men and women of God today have been trained through practically serving another Christian leader for years before the Lord opens up a door of public ministry or leadership for them.

In fact, Jesus Himself spent 30 years in His father's carpentry shop—in the ministry of helps. Stephen and Philip were powerful evangelists; however, they both were also involved in serving tables (see Acts 6:1-7). I encourage you to ask yourself, "How can I serve a leader whom the Lord has placed in my life?" Tell him or her that you are willing to serve in the ministry of helps as the Lord trains you for future ministry.

For years, I served in the ministry of helps in a youth outreach. We played basketball and other sports with young people so that we could share Christ with them. My responsibility in the basketball club was to bring the basketball and to be the chauffeur who brought the young people to the basketball court week after week. Some time later, I was asked to take a small group of new believers and start a believers' Bible study. The Lord used these acts of serving in my life to train me for future ministry.

If you want to find your ministry, a place to start is by serving in the ministry of helps as prescribed in the Word of God. Often, those people who try to push themselves into the limelight are the very ones who need to serve behind the scenes where the Lord can work His heart of a servant into them. God desires to exalt us, but He asks us to humble ourselves first so that He can exalt us in due time (see 1 Pet. 5:6).

WE ARE CALLED TO SERVE
REFLECTION QUESTIONS

1. In what ways are servant-leaders exalted by the Lord?

2. Describe ways that you have served in the background.

3. How can you remain humble if you are recognized as an expert or authority on a subject?

4. What is the ministry of helps? Have you ever served in this kind of ministry? How?

Chapter 19

MINISTERING WITH COMPASSION

LOVING REGARDLESS OF THE RESPONSE

Whenever Jesus ministered to others, His ministry came from a heart of love and compassion: *"When He saw the crowds, He had compassion on them, because they were harassed and helpless, like sheep without a shepherd"* (Matt. 9:36).

Jesus loved the people He served and has called us to do the same. First Corinthians 13 is often known as the "love chapter" in the Bible. The Scriptures in this chapter teach us that we can do all kinds of good deeds and "ministry," but unless it is done from a heart of love, it will be of no profit for us or others.

Love is not just a feeling but a decision that you make. *Love is giving with no expectancy of return.* Jesus Christ loved us. He went to the cross and made a decision to love us, regardless of our response to Him. In the same way that Jesus gave His life for us, He has called us to love others and give our lives for them. We can love others because Jesus Christ loved us first. Since Christ lives in us, His love is in us. Every day we need to allow the love of God to be released in our lives. Either we live by what the Word of God says and by the truth of Christ living in us, or we live by our emotions and by the way that we feel. Here is an excellent checklist to use as you minister to others: *"But the wisdom that comes from heaven is first of all pure; then peace-loving, considerate, submissive, full of mercy and good fruit, impartial and sincere"* (James 3:17). If you want to give someone counsel, you can readily decide whether or not you have Christ's compassion by asking: "Am I willing to yield?" "Is the counsel I'm giving pure?" "Is it bringing peace, or is it bringing confusion?" *"God is not the author of confusion but of peace"* (1 Cor. 14:33 NKJV).

Many times we may say the right thing but with a wrong attitude. This will not produce the spiritual results that God desires. We can respond like a lamb or a snake to those around us. A lamb is willing to yield and even be taken to the slaughter (see Isa. 53:7). The devil will always rise up in resistance like a snake: "Who are *you* telling *me* what to do?" God has called us to respond to others and minister to them like a lamb—with love and compassion.

START SMALL

As we minister to others out of a heart of love and compassion, we need to recognize that there are many different kinds of ministries that the Lord has given to His people. First Corinthians 12:4-7,11 says:

> *There are diversities of gifts, but the same Spirit. There are differences of ministries, but the same Lord. And there are diversities of activities, but it is the same God who works all in all. But the manifestation of the Spirit is given to each one for the profit of all…. But one and the same Spirit works all these things, distributing to each one individually as He wills* (NKJV).

I have met people who feel that they are called to minister to others by singing or leading in worship when, in actuality, they cannot carry a tune. The Lord simply has not given them the ability to sing. We need more than an inward motivation for a spiritual gift; we also need to be enabled to perform it. God is the One who gives us the power to perform ministry of any kind. We will know when we are functioning in the ministry that God has given us because it will produce certain results.

A great place to begin to minister to others is in a small group setting such as a cell group or house church. Maybe God has called you to prophesy. Perhaps the Lord has given you a song to sing that would be a blessing to other believers. The place to start is in a small group of believers. When you are faithful in this smaller setting, the Lord can then release you in larger settings in the future.

Sometimes people have what may be called a "preacher's itch." They constantly think they are responsible to preach and teach at every meeting that they go to. Desiring to preach the Word is a very noble desire. However, ministry is serving. As was mentioned earlier, Stephen and Philip served tables, and then God released them as mighty evangelists. They started by practical service. We should follow their example.

WHAT COUNTS FOR ETERNITY

Many years ago, we spent much of our time ministering to a group of young people who grew up in homes without Christ. One day, some of these youngsters sat on our Volkswagen's sunroof, damaging it. From that time on, whenever it rained, water would leak from the roof and drip on my knee as I drove. For awhile, I had to watch my attitude. Was it really worth it to minister to these young, rowdy people who caused my car's sunroof to leak and showed no appreciation for what we did for them? Soon I realized, "What does it matter anyway?" All that matters is where these youngsters spend eternity. Today, some of those young people are dynamic Christians.

As we see life from God's perspective, we realize that all that really counts is our relationship with God and our relationship with others as we serve those around us. God's call on our lives is first to love Him and then to love people. Paul the apostle said in First Corinthians 9:22, *"To the weak I became weak, to win the weak. I have become all things to all men so that by all possible means I might save some."*

If we truly love people, we will do what it takes to relate to them, helping them come to know Jesus and fulfill the call of God on their lives. Many issues that we consider of major importance are really minor in God's eyes. Let's just love Jesus and one another and realize that we are ministers. Then let's reach out to those around us in His name. God is calling many kinds of people to become part of His Church, according to Galatians 3:28-29:

There is neither Jew nor Greek, slave nor free, male nor female, for you are all one in Christ Jesus. If you belong to Christ, then you are Abraham's seed, and heirs according to the promise.

I get excited when I go to a meeting of believers and see them loving and accepting one another. One person wearing a suit sits next to someone wearing an old pair of jeans. There are no social, national, racial, or gender distinctions with regard to our relationship with the Lord. It is not what is on the outside that is so important, but what is on the inside—a heart that is being changed by Jesus Christ.

GOD USES IMPERFECT PEOPLE

Let's take a moment and look at the kind of people that God calls into leadership to minister effectively to others. This may surprise you. Let's start with Moses. *"But Moses said to God, 'Who am I, that I should go to Pharaoh and bring the Israelites out of Egypt?' And God said, 'I will be with you...'"* (Exod. 3:11-12).

Moses didn't feel like he was capable to do the job that the Lord was asking him to do. Most Christians who are called to ministry feel the same way. They know they will have to rely on God's strength and not their own. The first small group Bible study that I ever led seemed like a monumental task, but I took a step of faith because I knew that God would give me the strength. Joshua was fearful when he responded to the Lord's call on his life. God told Joshua, *"Have I not commanded you? Be strong and courageous. Do not be terrified; do not be discouraged, for the Lord your God will be with you wherever you go"* (Josh. 1:9).

The Lord had to encourage Joshua continually in his new role as a leader. We do not depend on our ability but upon God's ability in us. If you feel like you do not have all of the natural gifts that you need to be able to minister to others effectively, be encouraged. You have a lot of company. Moses and Joshua and many others through-out the Scriptures felt the same way. But God used them anyway. The Bible tells us that God has chosen to use imperfect people to ful-fill His purposes, confounding the wisdom of those who seem to be wise in this world (see 1 Cor. 1:27).

DO NOT BE AFRAID

Gideon was another individual who struggled when the Lord called him to areas of ministry and leadership:

"But sir," Gideon replied, "if the Lord is with us, why has all this happened to us? Where are all His wonders that our

fathers told us about...But now the Lord has abandoned us and put us into the hand of Midian."

The Lord turned to him and said, "Go in the strength you have and save Israel out of Midian's hand. Am I not sending you?"

"But Lord," Gideon asked, "how can I save Israel? My clan is the weakest in Manasseh, and I am the least in my family."

The Lord answered, "I will be with you, and you will strike down all the Midianites together" (Judges 6:13-16).

Have you ever felt like Gideon? You may know that the Lord has called you to minister, and yet when you look at your own "track record," you can hardly believe that it is possible that the Lord could use you. Yet if you seek to serve the Lord, He promises to be with you (see Matt. 28:19-20).

Jeremiah was another individual who felt the same way that many young people feel when they realize that God has called them to minister to others. Jeremiah, a young man, told the Lord in Jeremiah 1:6-8:

"Ah, Sovereign Lord...I do not know how to speak; I am only a child."

But the Lord said to me, "Do not say, 'I am only a child.' You must go to everyone I send you to and say whatever I command you. Do not be afraid of them, for I am with you and will rescue you," declares the Lord.

A feeling of "I can't do it" is a common thread that runs through each of these individuals' responses when the Lord called them to ministry and leadership. This is the type of person that the Lord will use—those who are completely dependent on Him. No matter what your task is in life, the Lord promises to be with you and help you.

Maybe you feel like you've made too many mistakes and the Lord can never use you again. Look at Jonah. After He ran from God and was swallowed by a great fish, the Bible states, *"Then the word of the Lord came to Jonah a second time"* (Jon. 3:1).

God is always the God of a second chance. We need to put all of our trust in Him. We must be convinced that, if God doesn't show up, it's all over. God has a "track record" of using those who feel like they cannot do the job. Remember, man looks at the outward appearance, but God looks at the heart (see 1 Sam. 16:7). When our heart is in the right place—completely submitted to Him—it is amazing what the Lord can do to equip us for the responsibilities that lie ahead.

CONNECTED AND PROTECTED

God's purpose in the earth today is to build His Church (see Matt. 16:18). His universal Church is made up of multitudes of local churches in every part of the world. Their goal is to preach the Gospel, bringing men and women into a saving relationship with Christ. Each and every local church should desire to motivate their members to reach out. The early church leaders in Antioch got together to fast and pray, and then sent out a dynamic missionary team:

In the church at Antioch there were prophets and teachers... While they were worshiping the Lord and fasting, the Holy Spirit said, "Set apart for Me Barnabas and Saul for the work to which I have called them." So after they had fasted and prayed, they placed their hands on them and sent them off (Acts 13:1-3).

Paul and Barnabas were not sent out on a lone mission; the church supported and encouraged this missionary team, and they reported back to the church telling all that had happened:

From Attalia they sailed back to Antioch, where they had been committed to the grace of God for the work they had now completed. On arriving there, they gathered the church together and reported all that God had done through them... (Acts 14:26-27).

This shows the importance of being sent out to minister from our local church and reporting back to them what the Lord is doing through us. God's desire is to continue to build His Church—the congregations of believers in your local community. Jesus told His disciples that the gates of hell will not prevail against the Church of Jesus Christ (see Matt. 16:18).

Sometimes, because of zeal or a lack of understanding of the Scriptures, Christians get excited about ministering to others without being properly connected to the local church. I have met various people through the years who have not been properly connected to the Body of Christ and have gone through many kinds of struggles that were unnecessary. As we minister to others, it is important to be properly connected and protected through the local church.

WE ARE ALL KINGS AND PRIESTS

Although we may find it hard to admit, at times we base our understanding of God on our preconceived ideas and our past experiences. Baptists grow up with a Baptist understanding of the Scriptures, and the same can be said of Methodists, Lutherans, Charismatics, and so forth. Depending on our church's denomination, we are convinced that our brand of theology is correct.

The truth is, we should be sure that what we believe is based on the Word of God and not on a distorted traditional understanding.

The Berean Christians refused to take everything that Paul preached at face value. They went home and studied the Scriptures to be sure that the things that Paul said were really true: *"...For they received the message with great eagerness and examined the Scriptures every day to see if what Paul said was true"* (Acts 17:11).

Is it possible that certain traditions that we consider to be completely scriptural are not based on the Bible at all? Could it be that the real reason we do certain things is because our spiritual parents and grandparents did them? I've heard the story of a young mother who always cut off the ends of a whole ham before baking it in the oven. When she was asked why she always followed this procedure, she said, "Because Grandma did it that way." Little did she know that grandma's roast pan was too small for the entire ham—that was the only motivation that grandma had to cut off the ends!

Some traditions are good; however, we need to be sure that our ways of thinking are the same as God's. I believe a poor tradition (unbiblical, unscriptural) in the Church has been the understanding that the pastor should do the entire ministry while the other believers simply come week after week to be fed. As we've learned from the Scriptures in this book, every saint is called to be a minister; otherwise, the Church will never be built as the Lord intended.

Many Christians today have elevated pastors of a local church as holy men who stand between them and the Lord. The Scriptures tell us He has made all of us kings and priests: *"And has made us kings and priests to His God and Father..."* (Rev. 1:6 NKJV).

We all have direct access to the Lord through the shed blood of Jesus Christ. Praise God for the pastors, elders, and spiritual leaders whom the Lord has placed in our lives, but we should not expect them to do the entire ministry. We are called by God to minister to others. Our spiritual leaders should encourage us, equip us, and train us to be servants who minister to others. Let's expect to be a minister today. Ask the Lord to open your eyes to see needs around you. Then expect the Lord to give you the grace and the strength to minister to others.

MINISTERING WITH COMPASSION
REFLECTION QUESTIONS

1. Name the things on the checklist of James 3:17 that will be evident as you minister to others.

2. How can you begin to allow the Lord to use you in your spiritual gift(s)? Do others recognize the gift(s) in you? How can you "become all things to all men" (see 1 Cor. 9:22)?

3. Describe any times when you felt inadequate to minister but the Lord gave you the grace to do it. What does the Lord promise in Joshua 1:9?

4. How are you connected to and protected by the Church? What can happen if you are not connected?

Chapter 20

WE ARE ON JESUS' TEAM

LIVE EACH DAY TO THE FULLEST

How would you feel if the president or prime minister of your nation personally asked you to serve on his or her team? I have even more awesome news for you—the King of the entire universe has handpicked you as one of His personal ministers! When we get up in the morning, rather than dreading the day ahead of us, we can be assured that God wants to use us as one of His ministers. As we go to work, to school, or to serve in our homes or communities, God has called us to be ministers. God orchestrates His plans in our lives so that we will meet people who need Jesus Christ and His ministry. As we trust Him in faith, He will unfold His plans before us.

One of the tricks of the enemy, aimed at trying to keep us from being fulfilled in God and in ministry, is to try to tempt us to live in the past. If that doesn't work, the enemy will tempt us to be overly concerned about our future. God wants us to live to the fullest in the present and to allow Him to reign in the midst of our problems. Matthew 6:33-34 tells us:

> But seek first His kingdom and His righteousness, and all these things will be given to you as well. Therefore do not

worry about tomorrow, for tomorrow will worry about itself. Each day has enough trouble of its own.

Every problem that you have is an opportunity for a miracle. As you read through the Bible, you'll find that every miracle was preceded by a problem. The Red Sea parted because the children of Israel had a problem—they had to flee the pursuing Egyptians. Jesus fed the 5,000 because there was a problem—the people were hungry. The blind man was healed because he had a problem—he could not see. God desires to use you as an instrument of His miraculous power.

Some time back, I was talking to a small group of people and I felt an impression from the Lord that one of the ladies was living with a fear that had been tormenting her for many years. As I shared this with her and the others in the room, she began to cry. We prayed for her, and Jesus ministered His peace and healing. Keep your eyes open; there are needs all around you. You can speak words that bring life to others.

EXPECT JESUS TO USE US

Some Christians believe that they need to have their whole life planned out for them. But really, the way to live for Jesus is one day at a time. Life is much like a football game. The football coach cannot possibly plan out every play because every play is dependent on the plays that the opposing team will make. In the "game of life," the enemy has plans, and God has plans. We stand in the middle of the playing field. Let's trust Jesus day by day and minute by minute and expect Him to use us to minister to others. He has the ultimate plan.

When we learn to fellowship with the Lord and listen to His voice, we will realize that He is always at work around us. Jesus said:

> *...My Father is always at His work to this very day, and I, too, am working....I tell you the truth, the Son can do nothing by Himself; He can do only what He sees His Father doing, because whatever the Father does the Son also does. For the Father loves the Son and shows Him all He does. Yes, to your amazement He will show Him even greater things than these* (John 5:17,19-20).

What is God the Father doing around you right now? Let's find out what the Father is doing and then partner with Him as one of His vital ministers. Remember—God is the initiator; we are the responders: *"No one can come to Me unless the Father who sent Me draws him..."* (John 6:44).

God is drawing people to Jesus Christ. Let's watch, pray, and then respond as the Holy Spirit leads us to minister to others.

MINISTER OUT OF HIS LOVE

Never forget—even though it is important to minister to others, God desires a personal love relationship with each of us. He really loves us. How can we know that Jesus loves us? Because He laid down His life for us at the cross 2000 years ago. Jesus loves us as much as the Father loves Him!

> *As the Father has loved Me, so have I loved you. Now remain in My love. If you obey My commands, you will remain in My love, just as I have obeyed My Father's commands and*

remain in His love....Greater love has no one than this, that he lay down his life for his friends (John 15:9-10,13).

My daughter once prayed with a young lady in another nation. "Do you love Jesus?" she asked her. "Oh yes," the young lady responded, "but I do not love God the Father." She went on to explain that her father had molested her and that, because of this devastating experience, she could not trust the Father in Heaven. My daughter explained to her that God, our heavenly Father, loves her perfectly.

As we minister to others, we need to minister out of an understanding that God loves us. We never should minister to *be* accepted by God or others. We minister because we *are* accepted by God, and we are able ministers of His love. In Isaiah 43:4, God expresses His love for Israel: *"Since you are precious and honored in My sight, and because I love you...."*

That same love applies to you and me today. God really loves you! He has redeemed us, and we belong to Him. As we experience this love, we then can effectively minister that love to those around us. Lovers tell one another every day that they love each other. We need to tell our God how much we love Him. Jesus has told us in His Word over and over again how much He loves us. We can be effective in ministering to others as we experience our God's acceptance and love in our own lives.

PARTNER WITH JESUS

We are privileged to partner together with God and be involved in what He is doing on the earth today. The Bible tells us in John 15:16, *"You did not choose Me, but I chose you and appointed you...."*

God chose to use us. When I was a young boy, I played baseball with my schoolmates. However, since I was not a very good baseball player, sometimes I was not chosen for the team. I can remember standing in a row of young boys, waiting to be picked to play on the team. It felt so good when I was chosen. God wants you to know that He has chosen you to serve on His team. He has appointed you to bear fruit for Him.

Everywhere you go this week, ask Jesus, "Lord, what are You doing around me? Open my spiritual eyes to see as You see. I know that You love me, so how do You want me to be involved in Your work this week?" Maybe He wants you to give an encouraging word to someone or to write them a note. Perhaps the Lord will lead you to pray for someone who needs to be encouraged and strengthened. The Lord may call you to minister to some children or listen to someone who has been going through a stressful time in his or her life.

I don't know why God chooses to use people, but He does. If I was God, I probably would not have chosen to use people. We make so many mistakes as human beings. But God chooses to use us for His purposes on this planet. Let's remain secure in His love for us so that we can minister effectively to others in His name.

DECIDE TO OBEY

In order to be effective as a believer in Jesus Christ, we need to make a decision every day to obey Him as His ministers. Paul wrote to the Corinthian church encouraging them to obey the Lord in everything, no matter what came their way: *"The reason I wrote you was to see if you would stand the test and be obedient in everything"* (2 Cor. 2:9).

Life is a series of decisions. Today you will make decisions that may affect the rest of your life. Let's be sure to acknowledge the Lord constantly in all of our decision-making so that we can truly partner with Jesus to be His ministers.

Naaman, in the Old Testament, desiring to be healed, came to the prophet Elisha (see 2 Kings 5). Elisha told him to wash in the Jordan River seven times. At first he reacted negatively, but then he made a decision, at the prompting of his servants, to obey the voice of the prophet. As he washed in the Jordan River, he was made whole. Obedience paid off for Naaman.

It always pays to be obedient. Every day, you and I have the opportunity and privilege to be ministers to others. The enemy will try to cause us to be self-centered and to think only of ourselves and our own needs and problems. However, when we make a decision each day to be a partner with Jesus, life takes on a whole new meaning.

I'm very grateful to those who have ministered to me. I'm grateful for the young lady who told me about Jesus Christ many years ago. I'm grateful for a pastor who was patient with me and ministered to me when I was baptized with the Holy Spirit. I'm grateful for my parents and others who provided for me when I was a young boy as they ministered to me in practical ways. I'm grateful for other believers who have encouraged me. The Bible tells us that much will be required of those who receive much (see Luke 12:48). God has been very good to us. He now requires us to minister to others. Let's make a decision today to do it.

PLEASE GOD RATHER THAN MAN

As you reach out in faith and minister to others, you will find that there will be times when you will be misunderstood. For example, when Jesus ministered healing to the blind man, both Jesus and the man who was healed were misunderstood. When the religious leaders asked the blind man if he thought Jesus was a sinner or not, he replied, *"...Whether he is a sinner or not, I don't know. One thing I do know. I was blind but now I see!"* (John 9:25).

This man refused to defend himself. He simply spoke the truth. When you and I choose to obey the living God and minister to others in Jesus' name, we should not be surprised if there are times when we are misunderstood. Remember—it is God whom we serve first, not man. We will find that everyone will not always understand. Jesus and His apostles were misunderstood many times. In fact, Paul the apostle writes, *"Am I now trying to win the approval of men, or of God? Or am I trying to please men? If I were still trying to please men, I would not be a servant of Christ"* (Gal. 1:10).

Pleasing God must be our top priority. If we desire to please people rather than please God, we are no longer effective as ministers of Jesus Christ. When I was baptized with the Holy Spirit, many people misunderstood—even well-meaning people. Sometimes, when I have the privilege of leading people to faith in Jesus Christ, their friends and family members have been upset at me. But this is the price that we may have to pay as believers in Jesus Christ who are called to minister to others.

When we minister to others, we are called to love them and speak in a way that brings God's peace and blessing on them: *"If it is possible, as far as it depends on you, live at peace with everyone"* (Rom. 12:18). However, we cannot focus on pleasing others more than pleasing Jesus. The early apostles declared boldly, *"We must obey God rather than men"* (Acts 5:29).

GOD HAS CHOSEN YOU

One of the greatest ways for us to experience and continue to build a love relationship with the Lord is to partner with Him. He desires to do His greater works through us:

> *I tell you the truth, anyone who has faith in Me will do what I have been doing. He will do even greater things than these, because I am going to the Father. And I will do whatever you ask in My name, so that the Son may bring glory to the Father. You may ask Me for anything in My name, and I will do it* (John 14:12-14).

During the year that LaVerne and I were engaged to be married, we spent much of our time in ministry to young people. As we partnered together in ministry, the Lord allowed us to get to know one another better. This same concept is true in our relationship with our Lord Jesus. As we partner with Jesus and minister to others, we will continue to get to know Him more intimately.

Keep your "spiritual eyes" open. What is Jesus doing in your life, in the lives of your loved ones, or in the lives of those He has placed around you? How has He called you to partner with Him to minister to and serve others? Expect the Lord to use you today, and remember: "...*We have this treasure in jars of clay to show that this all-surpassing power is from God and not from us*" (2 Cor. 4:7).

We have the treasure, our Lord Jesus Christ, within us. The power that we have to minister to others is not of us—it is from Him. We are weak "jars of clay," but Jesus lives powerfully within our human weakness.

When you lay hands on sick people and pray, expect them to recover. Christ lives in you. As you speak words of encouragement to others, expect the Lord to use you to boost their faith. And never forget—God, the King of the whole universe, has chosen *you* as one of His choice ministers!

WE ARE ON JESUS' TEAM
REFLECTION QUESTIONS

1. When you speak words of encouragement to others, what happens?

2. How do you obey Jesus in your decision-making?

3. Have you ever endeavored to live at peace with someone but had to obey God first? What happened?

4. Describe a time when you felt weak, but the Lord gave you strength in your human weakness.

PART VI

The Great Commission

Chapter 21

WHAT IS THE GREAT COMMISSION?

GO AND MAKE DISCIPLES

A fter Jesus had risen from the dead and was ready to go back to His Father in Heaven, He called His 12 disciples together and gave them some last-minute instructions. We often refer to this as the "Great Commission." We read about it in Matthew 28:18-20:

> *Then Jesus came to them and said, "All authority in heaven and on earth has been given to Me. Therefore go and make disciples of all nations, baptizing them in the name of the Father and of the Son and of the Holy Spirit, and teaching them to obey everything I have commanded you. And surely I am with you always, to the very end of the age."*

Wouldn't you like to have been there when Jesus gave these last-minute "marching orders" to His disciples? Even though He would leave them to go to be with His heavenly Father, He promised to be with the disciples to the end.

Their mission on earth would be to make disciples in all nations. Jesus still gives this commission to us today. As disciples of Jesus Christ, our marching orders are to go and make disciples.

A *commission* is *a set of orders or instructions*. Jesus' instruction to go and make disciples of all of the nations is a commission—not an option. Some Bible scholars tell us that the word *go,* when translated from the original Greek language, implies "having gone."[1] In others words, as we live our lives for Jesus Christ, God has already called us to make disciples wherever we are. We may fulfill this call on the job, in our families, in our communities, in the Church, or on the mission field. Everywhere we go, we are called to make disciples.

In this chapter, we will learn what it means to go as a spiritual force (army) to evangelize, make disciples, mentor others, and see the Kingdom of God advance. We will discover that an effective way of making disciples is by mentoring others in a spiritual father or mother capacity. Spiritual fathers and mothers are those who gently help, develop, and encourage those they mentor to walk the path of becoming spiritual fathers and mothers themselves. Training through mentoring challenges all believers to both have and become spiritual parents, thus producing lasting and far-reaching results. In fact, these Biblical Foundation books were written to serve as a tool for any believer who is willing and obedient to make disciples according to the plan of our Lord Jesus Christ.

REACH THE NATIONS

An important part of the Great Commission is sending missionaries to areas of the world that have never heard the good news of Jesus Christ. There are many groups of people in areas of the world who have never heard the Gospel. Christians are commanded by the Lord to reach people from all nations: *"therefore go and make disciples of all nations…"* (Matt. 28:19).

God has called us as believers in Jesus Christ to carry the Gospel to the ends of the earth. Missionaries are those who have heard the call of God to live out their witness for Jesus within another culture in a region of the world unfamiliar with the Gospel. They hear God's heart to carry the news of eternal salvation to those dying without truth. Missionaries want to express their faith in the language of the common person in the country in which they live. They go into a nation, learn to speak the language, and live among the people to explain the Gospel and love people as they are drawn into the Kingdom of God.

A person called to be a missionary wants to see the Gospel penetrate the hearts of people and transform the societies in which they live. As they live in their "adopted" nation, they reach out to those the Lord places in their lives. God is looking for men and women who will go as missionaries to live out their faith in Christ in their new surroundings. Perhaps God will use your life to bring the message of salvation to needy people in another country.

All of us are called to be involved in missions in some way. Some are called to go while others are called both to pray for missionaries and to support them financially. Ask the Lord to reveal His plan to you regarding world missions.

THE STRATEGY

The Great Commission of our Lord Jesus Christ is really very simple. It is a call to make disciples. You may ask, "How do we go to all of the world to make disciples?" We start right where we are! God has called us as His Church to touch every nation of the world, but we must ask the Lord where He has called us specifically. Although some believers will go to another country to make disciples, many believers will reach out to others right where they live. God places people all around us whom we can disciple and train.

Disciples are made one at a time. Jesus ministered to multitudes of people, but He spent most of His time with just 12 disciples. Jesus had different levels of relationships among those He ministered to. John was probably Jesus' closest friend, according to John 13:23. John was joined by Peter and James, another circle of intimate friends that Jesus had. The rest of the 12 disciples comprised another level of friendships for Jesus. Jesus also spent time with 70 of His disciples as well as with the 120 who witnessed Him ascending to His Father in Heaven (see Acts 1:15).

So then, in the same way that Jesus had levels of friendships, you will also have various spheres of friendships. The Lord desires for you to walk closely with a few people at a time so that you can "pour your life" into them. The Church of Jesus Christ is built through relationships, according to First Peter 2:5: "*You also, like living stones, are being built into a spiritual house....*" Each of us is a building stone for God to use in building His Kingdom. We are built together and held together by these God-ordained relationships.

God's intention is to raise up spiritual parents who are willing to nurture spiritual children and help them grow up in their Christian lives. A great evangelist was once asked what he would do if he wanted to impact a city. His plan was simplistic and strategic. He would find a few key men in the city, spend time with them, and literally pour his life into them, training them in the things that the Lord had shown him. As their spiritual father, he then would encourage each of these men to do the same—to find other men and to pour their lives into them. This is the essence of discipleship and spiritual parenting. The renowned evangelist believed that he could see an entire city affected for Christ through this strategy. I heartily agree. The Lord is bringing back the truth of discipleship and spiritual parenting to the Church of Jesus Christ.

RELATIONSHIPS LAST FOREVER

The Lord has called us to build relationships with one another. Relationships, although they may change, last forever. When you and I get to Heaven, all that is really going to count is the relationships that we have with God and with one another. Church buildings and church programs will crumble, but relationships last throughout eternity. The early Church met "house to house" so that they could experience family-type relationships to the fullest. Relationships were the key to the Kingdom of God as they met in each others' homes to nurture, equip, and serve each other:

> *So continuing daily with one accord in the temple, and breaking bread from house to house, they ate their food with gladness and simplicity of heart, praising God and having favor with all the people. And the Lord added to the church daily those who were being saved* (Acts 2:46-47 NKJV).

New people were continually added to the Church family because these early Christians practiced loving one another. They met in small groups so that disciples could be made more easily. More and more churches today utilize small groups because they are a place where everyone's gifts and talents can be exercised and experienced. In small groups, fellow Christians can pray for one another and experience God personally as they obey God's mandate to make disciples.

You see, making disciples does not just happen. Pray and ask God to show you those relationships that He desires for you to build so that you can "pour your life" into others and help them become mature believers in Jesus Christ. The Word of God has power to transform lives.

I am not ashamed of the gospel, because it is the power of God for the salvation of everyone who believes: first for the Jew, then for the Gentile (Romans 1:16).

For the message of the cross is foolishness to those who are perishing, but to us who are being saved it is the power of God (1 Corinthians 1:18).

The Gospel is powerful! Some people have a career of handling dynamite, knowing just how to blow holes in sides of mountains in order to construct roads. The explosive properties of dynamite, when used properly, are quite effective. We can be effective, too, when we realize that we can spread the Gospel, which will be explosive in a positive way in our communities, to change lives! During the Welsh Revival of the early 1900s, many police officers had nothing to do; crime had diminished due to the impact of the Gospel. The police force instead formed quartets and sang for community functions.

YOUR LIFE IS A BOOK

Paul the apostle instructed the early believers to follow his lifestyle as he followed Christ: *"Imitate me, just as I also imitate Christ"* (1 Cor. 11:1 NKJV).

People will imitate us when our lives imitate a love for God and others. They will be attracted to Jesus because of seeing His character in our lives. Do you know that the only spiritual book that some people ever read is your life? In fact, the Bible says in Second Corinthians 3:2-3:

> *You yourselves are our letter, written on our hearts, known and read by everybody. You show that you are a letter from Christ, the result of our ministry, written not with ink but with the Spirit of the living God, not on tablets of stone but on tablets of human hearts.*

In the Old Testament, the laws of God were written on the tablets of stone at Mount Sinai. But now, under the new covenant of Christ, the Holy Spirit writes God's law in people's hearts. This internal law consists of our love for God and others. People "read" our lives like a book. This is a tremendous privilege because we are modeling the Kingdom of God to those around us as people watch our lives.

If you are a parent, people watch how you relate to your children. If nonbelievers play sports with you, you have the privilege of showing them godly attitudes as you play. In your home, workplace, community, or school, people are watching to see if your life really exemplifies the principles of God. If they see you fail or make a mistake, they will hopefully also see you repent and make it right. People are looking for real Christians, not religious people who live by a legalistic set of man-made laws. They are looking for people with the love of God written on their hearts.

My life has been most profoundly changed through watching the example of others who have lived their Christian lives in front of me. Although I have enjoyed reading good books and listening to great preachers, the most powerful impact that Christ has had in my life comes from seeing Him modeled through other believers.

Sometimes those that I've been patterning my life after have made mistakes. But I've also seen their sincere repentance. Their example has spurred me on to *"love and good deeds"* (Heb. 10:24). I'm eternally grateful for those whom the Lord has placed around me to help me grow and be conformed to the image of Jesus Christ.

MINOR ON DIFFERENCES; MAJOR ON JESUS

One of the reasons many of God's people have lost sight of making disciples is because the enemy has deceived them, causing them to focus on problems and differences in the Church. We need to focus on Jesus and on making disciples. Matthew 6:33 tells us, *"But seek first His kingdom and His righteousness...."*

God's Kingdom is simply the King, Jesus Christ, and His domain. God is the ruler and the King of the whole universe. We are His servants and a part of His domain. His Kingdom includes every believer who names the name of Jesus Christ. It includes every congregation and family of churches who honor Him as Lord and believe in His Word.

His Kingdom has variety. When I have the opportunity to attend a family reunion, I am amazed at how different each of us looks, even with some common characteristics. Just as each family has its own distinctive characteristics, every congregation, denomination, or family of churches in God's Kingdom has its own distinguishing characteristics. Instead of majoring on the differences, the Lord's desire is for us to major on Jesus and the things that we can agree on.

For example, some Christians may have a personal conviction as to whether or not they should celebrate certain holidays. We must be careful that we do not allow these issues to divide us. The Bible tells us, *"One man considers one day more sacred than another; another man considers every day alike. Each one should be fully convinced in his own mind"* (Rom. 14:5).

We need to know what we believe about these minor issues and not be pressured by others into seeing these issues in exactly the same way. We should also be careful not to try to force everyone else to believe as we do on these minor issues.

SPIRITUAL UNITY

We are called to join together in unity to build His Kingdom. Let's focus on Jesus and on fulfilling His Great Commission. When we get to Heaven, we will probably all find out that we were wrong about certain things. It's reassuring to know that Jesus is committed to us, regardless! In Jesus' prayer for believers in John 17:20-21, He prays for their spiritual unity:

> *My prayer is not for them alone. I pray also for those who will believe in Me through their message, that all of them may be one, Father, just as You are in Me and I am in You. May they also be in Us so that the world may believe that You have sent Me.*

Our oneness is based on our common relationship to Jesus. We do not have to think exactly alike, but God wants His children to have the same basic attitudes toward God's truth as revealed in His Word. The devil has tried to divide the Church of Jesus Christ for generations. Do not allow the devil to use you to criticize His Church. Jesus Christ is coming back for a Church who is in love with Him and with one another. Our God is coming back for a spotless Bride: *"...to present her to Himself as a radiant church, without stain or wrinkle or any other blemish, but holy and blameless"* (Eph. 5:27).

Although the Church is far from perfect, we are being conformed into the image of Christ and becoming the spotless Bride that our Lord Jesus has called us to be.

PRAYER, EVANGELISM, AND DISCIPLESHIP

Jesus' life was characterized by the basic values of prayer, evangelism, and discipleship. These basic values remind me of a three-legged stool. I live in a farming community. Many of those who have grown up on a farm can remember their parents using a three-legged milking stool to sit on while milking the cows each morning and evening. Why were there only three legs on the stool? Because no matter where you sat the stool on the barn floor, it would always be stable.

In the same way, we believe that God has given His Church a three-legged stool of truth as He uses prayer, evangelism, and discipleship to build His Church. When we give our lives to help others by praying for them, reaching out to them, and discipling them, the Lord will make sure that we are blessed in return. In fact, the greatest way to be blessed is to do what the Scripture says in Luke 6:38: *"Give, and it will be given to you. A good measure, pressed down, shaken together and running over, will be poured into your lap. For with the measure you use, it will be measured to you."*

Ecclesiastes 11:1 tells us, *"Cast your bread upon the waters, for after many days you will find it again."* When you take the time and effort to reach out to disciple and mentor another person, it may look like you are throwing away your chance of having your own needs met, but when you sow into others' lives, you are promised to reap a return. Proverbs 11:25 says, *"...He who refreshes others will himself be refreshed."*

A friend once told us about a time when she was sick and needed to be healed. Instead of focusing on her own problem, she started to pray for someone else who needed healing. During the prayer, the Lord miraculously touched our friend's body and brought healing into her life. As she refreshed someone else, she was refreshed.

ENDNOTE

1. S. Devasagayam Ponraj, "Church Planting and the Great Comission," http://www.abcog.org/plant.htm (accessed 2 Oct 2008).

WHAT IS THE GREAT COMMISSION?
REFLECTION QUESTIONS

1. Where are we commissioned to carry the Gospel, according to Matthew 28:19? How can we practically obey the Lord to reach the world?

2. How are disciples made? Think of your spheres of friendships; how can you make disciples within those spheres?

3. Why is a small group a more effective setting for discipling than a larger group?

4. Who should we imitate (see 1 Cor. 11:1)? Describe a time when you saw Christ in someone and it influenced your life.

Chapter 22

GET READY FOR SPIRITUAL WARFARE

WE ARE A SPIRITUAL ARMY

Throughout the Scriptures, Christians are exhorted to be spiritual soldiers, fighting in spiritual battles. Imagine how absurd it would be if all you did in the army was go to meetings to learn how to be in the army. True soldiers do more than go to meetings. They have to endure hardship and suffering in the world: *"Endure hardship with us like a good soldier of Christ Jesus"* (2 Tim. 2:3). They engage in warfare.

Likewise, in God's Kingdom, we are called to be a spiritual army, willing to endure suffering and difficulties as we help other people come out of spiritual darkness into the Kingdom of light. The reason Christians get together in small groups or in larger church meetings is to be trained from the Word of God so that they can go out into the world as victorious spiritual soldiers. God has called us to help people come to know Jesus Christ.

The Church is like an army with a medical unit. If God's soldiers get wounded, they can receive healing and get back on the battlefield. As the Church, we can help people come to know Jesus Christ and grow in Him. God is building His Kingdom. His Kingdom is made up of many different churches, families of churches, and denominations who are called to work together throughout the world.

We must encourage other Christians to continue in the faith: *"…Encourage one another daily…"* (Heb. 3:13a). Let's encourage and strengthen one another so that we can stand together as a strong army, preparing for the return of our Lord Jesus. We are called to encourage members of the Body of Christ every day through cards, letters, phone calls, and acts of kindness. The devil lies to God's people by telling them that they are no good, that they will never fulfill the Lord's purpose for their lives. God wants us to build His people up. We counteract the lies of the devil by speaking the truth of God's Word to others and encouraging them.

In this chapter, we will look at the weapons of spiritual warfare that the Lord has given us as we accomplish the Great Commission.

THE PRAYER WEAPON

Spiritual warfare is real. The spirit world is real. Two major tactics of the enemy are: first, to make us believe that he is not real, and second, to produce an overemphasis on him. Some people choose to believe that the devil is just a fairy tale—a guy in a red costume with pointed ears and a tail. Just because we cannot see the devil does not mean that he is not real. We cannot see radar, radio waves, or nuclear radioactivity, but they are still very real.

Other people blame everything on demons and the devil. They overemphasize his power instead of the Lord's. We must keep our focus on Jesus, not on the enemy. Sometimes, instead of blaming everything on demons and the devil, we need to acknowledge that there may be an area in our lives that the Lord wants to discipline. We must continually war against those things that limit God's work in our lives.

How does a Christian wage war? We must be strong in the Lord and put on the whole armor of God to engage in our spiritual conflict with evil. We wage this spiritual warfare by the power of the Holy Spirit (see Rom. 8:13). Paul tells us in Ephesians 6:10-12 to put on spiritual armor, like soldiers, so that we can stand against satan's schemes:

> *Finally, be strong in the Lord and in His mighty power. Put on the full armor of God so that you can take your stand against the devil's schemes. For our struggle is not against flesh and blood, but against the rulers, against the authorities, against the powers of this dark world and against the spiritual forces of evil in the heavenly realms.*

Our fight is not with people; the real war is with the demons of hell, the angels of darkness. The only weapons to which they respond are spiritual weapons. Prayer is a powerful spiritual weapon against the powers of darkness. Second Corinthians 4:3-4a tells us, *"And even if our gospel is veiled, it is veiled to those who are perishing. The god of this age has blinded the minds of unbelievers, so that they cannot see the light of the gospel."*

Satan blinds the minds of people who do not believe. Those who do not submit themselves to Jesus are under satan's rule. He "veils" their eyes to the truth of the Gospel to keep them from believing in Jesus Christ. Imagine driving down a road and seeing a sign alerting you that a bridge is washed out. You immediately know that you should follow the detour. Now imagine a drunk driver seeing the same sign. With his impaired judgment, he may read the sign without truly comprehending the dangers. It is possible that he may drive off the edge of the bridge to his destruction because he was blinded to the truth. People all around us today are going to hell. The Bible makes it clear that we can pray and bind the powers of darkness in Jesus' name so that people will see the truth. Matthew 18:18 says, *"I tell you the truth, whatever you bind on earth will be bound in heaven, and whatever you loose on earth will be loosed in heaven."*

Jesus says that we can bind (tie up spiritually) the demonic strongholds that are in people's lives. There is power in prayer. As we bind these strongholds in Jesus' name, people will be set free to hear the Gospel and respond to Jesus Christ.

A young man once told me, "The only reason I am a Christian today is because my mother prayed for me." This mother understood the principles of the Kingdom of God. Let's get serious about praying for those whom the Lord has placed in our lives who need to draw closer to Jesus. We can bind the blinding spirits deceiving them so that they can understand and respond to the good news of Jesus Christ.

TRUTH KEEPS YOU GROUNDED

We saw in Ephesians 6:10-12 that before we wrestle with demonic strongholds (principalities and powers), we need to put on the whole armor of God. The next two verses mention the first piece of armor to put on:

> *Therefore put on the full armor of God, so that when the day of evil comes, you may be able to stand your ground, and after you have done everything, to stand. Stand firm then, with the belt of truth buckled around your waist...* (Ephesians 6:13-14a).

When Paul the apostle was writing this, he was sitting in a prison cell looking at the soldiers surrounding him. He was able to write from a spiritual perspective about what he saw in the natural realm. He was able to stand his ground in his day of trial. Some days may be very easy for you, and other days you may find yourself under intense attack from the devil. These attacks may come in the form of depression, oppression, fear, or confusion. When the "evil day" comes, we need to learn how to stand as good soldiers of Jesus Christ. If we do not stand firmly, we will get knocked off our feet. We must stand, having "truth buckled around our waist."

The Bible tells us that Jesus Christ is the way, the truth, and the life (see John 14:6). The armor and weapons strapped fast to the soldiers who guarded Paul in his prison cell were stabilized by a belt. This is why we need to have the spiritual belt of truth in place in our lives. We build everything in our Christian lives on the truth of the Word of God and on the truth of Jesus Christ.

Speak the truth of God's Word every chance you get. Quote the Scripture to yourself and to others. Remember, God's truth will set you free.

COVERING YOUR HEART AND FEET

As Christian soldiers, our spiritual armor includes a full suit. Ephesians 6:14b-15 continues on to name more spiritual pieces of armor to put on: "*...with the breastplate of righteousness in place, and with your feet fitted with the readiness that comes from the gospel of peace.*"

Righteousness refers to our *right standing with God*, which comes only by faith in Jesus Christ (see Rom. 4:3-5). Sometimes we may see ourselves through the eyes of our own mistakes. However, as we repent and come to the cross, God always sees us as righteous. He sees His Son, the Lord Jesus, the perfect lamb that was slain. Whenever we have a problem, the enemy will tell us that God is probably punishing us or that something is wrong with us. We must stand against the enemy in Jesus' name. We need to know we are righteous through faith in Jesus Christ.

We also need to make sure that our feet are fitted with the *"readiness that comes from the gospel of peace."* The Lord has called us to walk in peace with our God and with all men. The Bible tells us in James 3:18, *"Now the fruit of righteousness is sown in peace by those who make peace"* (NKJV). We can negotiate life's obstructions more easily if we attempt to live peaceably with others. If peace is broken, it doesn't matter whose fault it is; we are called to be peacemakers and to be reconciled to our brothers and sisters in Christ. If we need help, the Lord has provided the elders of the local church as mediators to help with these kinds of difficulties. We need to be ready and prepared to declare that the Gospel of Jesus Christ brings peace with God and peace with our fellow man.

If it is possible, as far as it depends on you, live at peace with everyone (Romans 12:18).

Therefore, if you are offering your gift at the altar and there remember that your brother has something against you, leave your gift there in front of the altar. First go and be reconciled to your brother; then come and offer your gift (Matthew 5:23-24).

The Lord asks us to do all that we can to pursue peace with others and then to trust Him to do the rest. Only God can change people's hearts and cause them to be reconciled.

HOLDING YOUR SHIELD OF FAITH

The piece of armor that a soldier really relied upon was the shield. The soldier's shield was a two foot by four foot shield behind which he stood in battle. It was an overall defense against attack because he could turn it in every direction to stop the arrows aimed at him: *"In addition to all this, take up the shield of faith, with which you can extinguish all the flaming arrows of the evil one"* (Eph. 6:16).

When you and I look at our circumstances, at times we can get discouraged. However, when we protect ourselves with our shield of faith and believe that God's Word is true, regardless of our circumstances, we can come through victoriously.

The fiery arrows of the enemy may include arrows of doubt, depression, condemnation, fear, or confusion. The list goes on and on. We need to keep up our spiritual shields so that when the enemy shoots arrows our way, we can respond with faith. Remember, *"...Faith comes by hearing, and hearing by the word of God"* (Rom. 10:17 NKJV). Let's speak forth the promises of the Word of God and not allow the fiery arrows of the evil one to burn a hole in our spiritual armor. We need to extinguish them quickly by speaking and believing the Word of God.

Even though we live in an instant society, we need to learn to live by faith. We may not always get results immediately, but we should continue to believe God's Word as truth, even in the midst of seemingly insurmountable circumstances. God is faithful. We can trust Him as we keep our shield of faith held high.

A few years ago, I met a lady whose son had strayed from the faith. While he was in rebellion, she continued to believe that God would speak to him. She knew that the Lord had given her a promise in Isaiah 59:21b: *"...My words that I have put in your mouth will not depart from your mouth, or from the mouths of your children...."* This mother chose to believe God's Word. As she kept her shield of faith high, her son was convicted by the Lord at an unlikely place—a rock-and-roll concert. Today he is a pastor. Remember, we live by faith and not by sight.

YOUR HELMET AND SWORD

Much of the Christian's battle is in the mind. Neither a Christian nor a soldier fighting a battle would fight very well if he did not have the hope of victory. We need to protect our heads with the helmet of salvation because the hope of salvation will defend our soul from the blows of the enemy. The helmet of salvation gives us the hope of continual safety and protection, built on the promises of God: *"Take the helmet of salvation..."* (Eph. 6:17a).

Remember, to be *saved* does not only mean *to be set free from sin and to live eternally with God*. Salvation also includes *healing, deliverance,* and *freedom from the powers of darkness*. I often travel to nations that do not have the same quality of medical expertise that we have in our western culture. I am amazed at the ability of God's people to truly believe Him for everyday miracles in these settings. It is impossible to figure out how miracles work. We simply accept by faith that God is a God of miracles. Our helmet of salvation keeps us from being confused by the powers of darkness and helps us to rely on God's great salvation and healing.

The Lord tells us to take up the final piece of armor—the sword of the Spirit. The sword was the only piece of armor that a soldier carried that was offensive as well as defensive. For a Christian, the sword of the Spirit is the powerful Word of God: *"...and the sword of the Spirit, which is the word of God. And pray in the Spirit on all occasions with all kinds of prayers and requests. With this in mind, be alert and always keep on praying for all the saints"* (Eph. 6:17b-18).

When we are armed with the truth of God's Word, the Holy Spirit living within us helps us to deal with temptations that come our way. We do not rely on our own wisdom, but on the Lord's. When we know His Word, we can withstand satan's lies. As we hide the Word of God in our hearts (see Ps. 119:11), we can resist sin.

The Bible tells us that the gates of hell will not prevail against the Church of Jesus Christ (see Matt. 16:18). As Christians, we are called to take over enemy territory. Do not settle for less. Take the Word of God seriously and confess it, believe it, live it, and expect to experience it in your life.

To be alert and to stand our ground, the Bible says that we must take up the whole armor of God (see Eph. 6:13). We must put on the belt of truth and the breastplate of righteousness. We prepare our-selves with the Gospel of peace and take up the shield of faith. In addition, we use the helmet of salvation and the sword of the Spirit. All of this armor is a protection and helps us to pray effectively. Paul the apostle says that we should pray always and be watchful as we pray for all of the saints. We are called to pray for one another. Spiritual warfare calls for intensity of prayer. It is not an option; it is a life and death matter.

READY FOR ACTION

We really do need to pray for one another. Prayer allows us to enter the conflict of spiritual warfare and to win the victory by working with God in this way. Paul the apostle asks for prayer in Ephesians 6:19-20 so that he can be bold in his witness for Christ:

Pray also for me, that whenever I open my mouth, words may be given me so that I will fearlessly make known the mystery of the gospel, for which I am an ambassador in chains. Pray that I may declare it fearlessly, as I should.

The Lord wants us to be bold witnesses for Jesus Christ, but boldness comes from our prayer closet. As we pray for those in our small groups, churches, youth groups, communities, homes, and workplaces, we will experience the boldness of the Lord to proclaim His Word to our generation. One time, while I was in the nation of Scotland, I found myself compelled to speak to a young man that I met on the street about Jesus. I knew that my boldness to speak out came because of prayer warriors who were praying for me.

If Paul the apostle needed others to pray for him to be bold, how much more do we need to be praying for one another to be bold today? In order for us to fulfill the Great Commission, we must be people of prayer. Remember to pray for missionaries whom the Lord has placed in your life to be bold for the Lord. And as we put on the full armor of God and pray each day, we will listen to our heavenly Father for orders from Heaven. Then we will experience Jesus using us to make disciples in our generation.

It has been my experience that most spiritual failure happens when Christians fail to keep their spiritual armor in place. When you get up in the morning, declare that you have placed the belt of truth around your waist. You are righteous through faith in Jesus Christ; the breastplate is in place. You have *"peace with God through [your] Lord Jesus Christ"* (see Rom. 5:1) because you are justified through faith. You walk in complete forgiveness toward anyone who's hurt you, and you have pursued peace with them as much as possible (see Rom. 12:18). You have taken up the shield of faith and will not allow the fiery darts of the enemy to hurt you. You will quench them in Jesus' name through faith in the Word of God. The helmet of salvation is secure. You know that you are born again and that Jesus Christ has changed your life. You take the Word of God and boldly, aggressively confront the powers of darkness in Jesus' name. You pray as a soldier who has properly placed the armor that the Lord Jesus has given you. You are ready for action! The world is waiting for us to declare the truth that will set them free.

GET READY FOR SPIRITUAL WARFARE
REFLECTION QUESTIONS

1. How often should we encourage each other, according to Hebrews 3:13? How do you encourage others?

2. In what ways does the devil attempt to knock you off your feet and make you ineffective in battle? How does God's Word, His truth, keep you stable?

3. How do we obtain righteousness? How can you be a peacemaker? Explain.

4. How do we defend ourselves from satan's "flaming arrows"?

Chapter 23

REACHING THE LOST AND MAKING DISCIPLES

TRUE EVANGELISM

God places a much higher priority on evangelism than we usually do. Why? Because God truly loves people: *"God so loved the world..."* (John 3:16). As Christians, we often become ingrown, looking within instead of trying to find ways to help people around us. God has called us to look outward. God's heart is for the world—for people. Evangelism is sharing the good news of Jesus Christ with others.

Many times Christians have a warped understanding of what evangelism really is. Some think that evangelism means they must knock on doors and pass out Gospel tracts. Although this can be an effective way to share your faith, the Lord may not call you to evangelize in that way. To others, evangelism means going to crusades. Praise God for crusades, but for most Christians, crusade evangelism is not the type of evangelism they are called to.

I believe that evangelism for most people will mean being so filled with Jesus that, wherever they go, they discover people who need a relationship with God. Our responsibility is to share with people what God has done in our lives and to encourage them to receive the good news of Jesus Christ into their lives.

In the story of the Good Samaritan (see Luke 10:33-37), the Samaritan found a man lying in the gutter and helped him, even though some of the religious folks of his day passed on by without lending a hand. The Samaritan practiced the principles of the Kingdom of God by loving the person God brought onto his path. Jesus made it very clear that we should *"love the Lord... [and] love your neighbor as yourself"* (Luke 10:27).

Loving God is a call to love others. Compassion for the lost and those in need is a sign that we really love God. After Jesus told the story of the Good Samaritan, He quizzed a nearby religious leader:

"[Who] was a neighbor to the man who fell into the hands of robbers?" The expert in the law replied, "The one who had mercy on him." Jesus told him, "Go and do likewise" (Luke 10:36-37).

We must operate in mercy and love. In Luke 15, Jesus gave three more stories about loving those around us. The first story was the parable of the lost sheep. Out of 100 sheep, one got lost, and the shepherd searched until he found it. The second parable involved a lost coin. The owner of the coin looked all day for it, putting all his effort into finding it. The third story is that of a prodigal son who took half of his father's fortune and left home to do his own thing. The Bible tells us that his father waited for him and then reached out lovingly when his son returned.

You see, God places a high priority on people who are hurting or lost. God has called us to reach out to those around us, even the "unlovely," so that He can fulfill His purposes through us. Jesus has called us to be fishers of men: *"'Come, follow me,' Jesus said, 'and I will make you fishers of men'"* (Mark 1:17).

Let's learn together how we can "catch men" and lead them to faith in Jesus Christ.

THE *OIKOS* PRINCIPLE

How did Jesus and the early Church lead people to faith? We sometimes call this the "*oikos* principle." The Greek word *oikos* means *household* or *family*.[1] Our *oikos* includes those with whom we relate on a regular basis. *Oikos* refers to one's personal community or those we are in relationship with.

The Scriptures tell us in Acts 10 that there was a man named Cornelius—a devout man who feared God along with his entire household, gave generously to the poor, and prayed to God regularly. One day Cornelius received a supernatural visitation from God through a vision. God told him to send messengers and call for Peter who would give him a message from God. Peter came to meet Cornelius who was "*...expecting them and had called together his relatives and close friends*" (Acts 10:24). Cornelius invited his *oikos* (relatives and friends) to this meeting with Peter, and many of those people came to know Jesus Christ.

Another story showing how God used someone's *oikos* to bring people to Jesus occurs in Acts 16. Paul and Silas were in prison when an earthquake opened all of the doors. The jailer was going to kill himself because he thought that the prisoners would escape and that he would be held responsible. Paul told him to refrain from harming himself because all the prisoners were safe. When Paul shared the Word of God with the jailer, his entire *oikos* (household) came to know Jesus Christ. All of us have people who have been placed in our lives by the Lord. They are the people with whom we can share the Gospel most effectively and easily. No matter where we live in the world, the *oikos* strategy of building by relationship is the most natural way of fulfilling the Great Commission. People want the truth. They are waiting for Christians they can trust to give them the truth.

You may want to list your *oikos* members on a sheet of paper. Pray and ask God to show you two or three people to focus on; begin to pray for these people and reach out to them. If they are unsaved, you will be involved in evangelism. If they are struggling in their Christian lives, God may call you to be involved in discipleship by becoming a spiritual father or mother to them.

The Scriptures tell us in the Book of Acts that new believers were *added* to the Church daily as they were being saved (see Acts 2:47). However, as we continue to read the Book of Acts, we see the Lord taking the Church another step. God's people began to grow in numbers. *"Then the churches throughout all Judea, Galilee, and Samaria had peace and were edified. And walking in the fear of the Lord and in the comfort of the Holy Spirit, they were multiplied"* (Acts 9:31 NKJV).

God's will is for us to be *multiplying* ourselves. In order for us to multiply, we need to get our eyes off of ourselves and to reach out to those who need to experience the life and power of Jesus Christ. We will see God's Kingdom expand and our own spiritual growth accelerate. Jesus spent His time here on this earth doing two things—talking to God about people and talking to people about God. He has called us to do the same.

KINDS OF PEOPLE IN YOUR *OIKOS*

There are several groups of people in our *oikos* or personal community. First of all, there are family members and relatives. Your

Uncle Jack and Aunt Sally are all part of your *oikos*, even if they live far away. If you maintain regular contact with them, they are part of your *oikos*. Second, those who share common interests with you are part of your *oikos*. They may play sports with you or share an interest in computers, or sewing. The list goes on. Third, those who live in your geographical location are part of your *oikos*—this, of course, includes your neighbors.

Those with whom you share a common vocation—your fellow employees—would fit into a fourth category. The fifth area would include those people with whom you have regular contact, including your dentist, family doctor, auto mechanic, sales people, school officials, classmates, and so on. People in your *oikos* group will be much more receptive to the Gospel because they trust you—you have built a relationship with them.

When Levi invited Jesus for dinner, he invited his *oikos* members or business associates. Luke 5:29 tells us of this occasion: *"Then Levi held a great banquet for Jesus at his house, and a large crowd of tax collectors and others were eating with them."*

Because Levi already had a relationship with them, these tax collectors gladly came to listen to what Jesus had to say. Jesus had the opportunity to share with members of Levi's *oikos,* and they were presented with the hope that Jesus offered. When we invite our *oikos* to meet Jesus, they have the opportunity to be presented with the truth that will set them free.

Nathanael was Philip's *oikos* member; they lived in the same town. Through their friendship, Philip led Nathanael to faith in Jesus Christ. The Bible tells us in John 1:45 that *"Philip found Nathanael and told him, 'We have found the one Moses wrote about in the Law, and about whom the prophets also wrote—Jesus of Nazareth...'"*

The Scriptures are filled with examples of people who came to know Jesus through someone with whom they had a relationship. Some time back, a small group leader in our church received a phone call from a woman in his small group. "Do you have any holy water?" he was asked. The group leader did not grow up in a Roman Catholic tradition and was not expecting this type of request. When he asked her for further details, she shared her concern for her daughter and her daughter's boyfriend. Strange things were happening in their home. An object had jumped off the stove and other unexplainable supernatural things were happening in their house. "May I come over to your daughter and her boyfriend's home to pray?" he asked.

"Oh yes," she explained, "and I want to be there when you come." The small group leader and his wife went over to the young couple's home to pray. After a time of sharing the Word of God, the young man received Jesus Christ as Lord. His girlfriend also expressed a desire to follow the Lord, and they were married a short time later. The demonic occurrences in their home stopped when the couple was set free spiritually. It all happened through a small group *oikos* relationship that expanded to include family *oikos* relationships. *Oikos* evangelism has a way of multiplying outward!

SPEND TIME MENTORING OTHERS

Jesus Christ called us to make disciples. The key to making disciples can be found in Mark 3:14-15a: *"He appointed twelve...that they might be with Him and that He might send them out to preach and to have authority...."*

Jesus was looking for 12 men with whom He could spend time so that He could show them the principles of the Kingdom of God. He wanted His disciples to experience God's principles as He modeled these truths for them through His own life. Discipleship often involves this kind of training through mentoring or modeling.

Jesus reached out to the disciples for companionship and training so that they might, in turn, go out to minister themselves. Discipling others means caring for them as friends and training them to grow in their Christian lives. Making disciples is not about telling other people what to do. Making disciples means literally laying down our lives for others and taking the time needed to see them grow spiritually. We can pray for, encourage, and help others focus on the Word of God, which gives clear instructions on how we should live our lives in Christ.

Biblical discipleship reminds me of serving as a coach for a sports team. The coach's responsibility is to help his players to be the best that they can possibly be. Unless we are reaching out and helping others, we become stagnant and ingrown. Like an ingrown toenail, pain will eventually occur. God has called us to reach out to others and to train them at the same time.

The Dead Sea is a world-renowned "stagnant" sea. Waters run into it, but nothing runs out. There is life in a river, but a sense of death remains in a stagnant pool. When we give out to others, the power and life of God will flow freely through our lives.

LEARN AND TEACH BY EXAMPLE

I love to play the guitar. I have had the privilege of teaching many others to play the guitar over the years. In fact, many of my students now play the guitar much better than I do. If I taught you how to play the guitar, I would sit down with you and a guitar. I'd show you how to play by teaching you exactly where to hold your fingers on the frets and how to hold the pick as you began to strum.

The same principle applies to the Kingdom of God. We are called to train, love, and show others how to become disciples of Jesus Christ. You may say, "Larry, I have only been a Christian for less than a year." Great! You can begin to show others what you have learned in the past year. God wants us to immediately reach out to those around us and to help them come into the Kingdom. The good news is that we don't have to know all of the answers. God is the One who has the answers. We can freely share with others that we don't have all of the answers, but that our God does. In fact, the Bible tells us in Deuteronomy 29:29, *"The secret things belong to the Lord our God, but the things revealed belong to us and to our children forever, that we may follow all the words of this law."*

The Bible makes it clear that we are responsible to act on those things that have been revealed to us by the Lord. Even when we don't have the answers to some of life's problems, the Lord will bring into our lives spiritual fathers or mothers who will be used by the Holy Spirit to help and guide us. Then the Lord will help us to do the same—to serve others and be a spiritual father or mother to them. As we work together, we can see God's Kingdom built as dozens and hundreds of lives in our communities are changed through the power of Jesus Christ.

Imagine, for a moment, every Christian you know training two or three others in the basic truths and experiences of walking with Jesus. These "disciples" would be encouraged to do the same. The results would be astounding. In fact, if you and I each discipled another believer every six months and encouraged each person we disciple to do the same, and the pattern was repeated every six months, in less than 30 years, the entire population of the world could be won to Christ!

HOSPITALITY IN HOMES

Do you know that one of the most powerful ways that we can be involved in discipleship and evangelism is through hospitality? Hospitality is a biblical principle that simply means *cheerfully sharing food and shelter and spiritual refreshment with those that God brings into our lives.* First Peter 4:9 tells us, *"Offer hospitality to one another without grumbling."*

I believe that the Lord wants to use our homes to build His Church. Our homes are to be used as places where people can be encouraged, filled with the Holy Spirit, and come to know Jesus Christ. The presence of God is in your home because Jesus Christ lives in you.

Because Christ lives in you, you can be assured that every place where you go, the presence of God will be there—in your home, at school, at the local restaurant, or at the store. God's Kingdom can be built as we eat breakfast with another person, laugh together, cry together, or just have fun sharing life together. The principle of hospitality can be a tremendous blessing as we make disciples and fulfill the Great Commission.

The Book of Acts opens and closes in a home. Homes are so important to the work of the Kingdom of God. The pastor of a very large church was asked the question, "Where is God's address?" His answer was that God's address is *our* address. In other words, God lives inside of you and me. Wherever you live, wherever you are, that is where God is. There are many people who would not feel free to go to a church meeting, but they would talk to you while sitting in your house eating a meal or playing a game in your living-room.

Romans 12:13 tells us that we should *"practice hospitality."* You may think, "My home is not nice enough to invite people in." Be assured, when people come into your home, they will sense the presence of God because He lives in you—they won't care about your house. When my wife, LaVerne, and I were first married, much of our hospitality was in a tiny mobile home. We had people coming in and staying overnight, eating with us, and praying with us, and they did not care that it was small. Expect the Lord to use your home, no matter what size, to build His Kingdom.

SOWING SPIRITUAL SEEDS

Praying, reaching the lost, and making disciples is a bit like sowing seed in a garden. When we sow spiritual seeds into people's lives through prayer, encouragement, and discipleship, we expect to get a crop eventually. We sow that seed in faith.

If I go out to my garden and dig up the seed every day and say, "I don't think it's growing," I will never get a crop. In the same way, we sow the truth of God's Word into people's lives in faith, knowing that, regardless of what we see today, we will get a crop in due time. We know, because we sowed our seeds in faith.

The Scriptures tell us in Mark 4 that, when we sow the seed of the Word of God into people's lives, several things can happen. For one, individuals may hear God's Word but fail to respond to it because satan immediately steals it away (see Mark 4:15). It is at these times that we should bind demonic activity in seekers' lives so they can be free to hear and accept God's Word.

The Scriptures also tell us that some people will hear the Word of God and immediately receive it with gladness. However, their roots are shallow, and they only endure for a time. When they go through hard times, they immediately stumble (see Mark 4:16-17).

Others may hear the Word but allow the things of this world to get in the way of their commitment to Christ:

Still others, like seed sown among thorns, hear the word, but the worries of this life, the deceitfulness of wealth, and the desires for other things come in and choke the word; making it unfruitful (Mark 4:18-19).

Because of the worries of this life, these people may find the Word of God being choked from their lives. If we sow seeds of encouragement into their lives and pray for them, we can keep the spiritual thorns from choking the Word of God out of their lives. They need some extra assistance during this time. Do you know that some varieties of trees, when first planted, need to have a stake driven into the ground next to the tree? A rope then is tied around the tree and stake until the tree can grow tall and strong enough to hold itself. God has called you and me to be "stakes" for people, helping to stabilize their lives until they can make it on their own.

Finally, there are those who hear God's Word and believe and persevere. They will bear fruit according to Mark 4:20: "*Others, like seed sown on good soil, hear the word, accept it, and produce a crop—thirty, sixty or even a hundred times what was sown.*"

As the Spirit of God, through us, pours His Word into people's lives, we are going to see a mighty harvest of people coming to know Jesus Christ. Someday we are going to stand before the Lord accompanied by multitudes of others—they are the result of the seeds that were sown—multiplying in numbers by the grace of God.

Have you ever heard of Mordecai Ham? Very few people have heard of him, and yet he has had a profound effect on the nations of the world. While Mordecai was preaching at a revival meeting in a tent, a young man came one evening and gave his life to Jesus. That man's name was Billy Graham.[2] Every person who has come to know Jesus Christ through Billy Graham's ministry is a product of the obedience of a man named Mordecai Ham.

D.L. Moody, a hundred years ago, was responsible for leading more than a million people to Jesus Christ. Yet the man who shared the Gospel with Mr. Moody was a common, ordinary man who made a decision to share Christ with the young boys in his Sunday school class.[3] The Bible says that the mustard seed is the smallest of all seeds, but it grows to be a majestic tree (see Matt. 13:31-32). As we are obedient to God in the "little areas," the Lord promises a great spiritual harvest.

The Great Commission is simply sowing seed. Good spiritual seed is sown through prayer, encouragement, and by sharing the Word of God with others. As we continue to sow in obedience, the seed will grow. The multiplication process will continue on and on. Healthy Christians are those who pray and reach out to those whom God brings into their lives. Let's rise up in faith together and labor with Jesus to fulfill the Great Commission.

ENDNOTES

1. *The New Testament Greek Lexicon*, s.v. "Oikos," www.studylight .org/lex/grk/view.cgi?number=3624 (accessed 2 Oct 2008).

2. "Who Led Billy Graham to Christ and Was it Part of a Chain of Conversions Going Back to Dwight L. Moody?" *Billy Graham Center*, www.wheaton.edu/bgc/archives/faq/13.htm (accessed 15 Sept 2008).

3. Hy Pickering, "Conversion of D.L. Moody: Prince of Evangelists," *Christian Biography Resources*, http://www.wholesomewords.org/biography/biomoody5.html (accessed 2 Oct 2008).

REACHING THE LOST AND MAKING DISCIPLES
REFLECTION QUESTIONS

1. What does evangelism mean to you? How did Jesus evangelize?

2. What does *oikos* mean? List people in your *oikos*.

3. List some practical ways that you can make yourself available to train disciples.

4. What does faith have to do with planting seeds in others' lives?

Chapter 24

BEING A SPIRITUAL FATHER OR MOTHER

THE NEED

Jesus invested three years of His earthly ministry into the lives of 12 men. It was valuable time spent fathering His spiritual children. This time of mentoring prepared and equipped the disciples to "go into all the world" and fulfill the Great Commission.

I briefly mentioned the concept of spiritual fathering and mothering earlier in this book. While discipleship is similar, in that it involves a few people getting together and helping the younger Christian, spiritual parenting has a much wider scope. Spiritual parenting has the intention of developing and encouraging others to walk the path of becoming spiritual fathers and mothers themselves. The spiritual father or mother mentors and trains another, and in doing so, imparts his or her inheritance to the younger Christian.[1]

New Christians desperately need spiritual fathers or mothers to nurture and encourage them in their spiritual walk. The man who served as a pastor in my church for many years told me that, when he received Christ, he was in his mid-20s. A 77-year-old "spiritual father" from his church took him under his wing and discipled him. It made all the difference for this future pastor's spiritual maturity.

Paul the apostle told the Corinthian church that they should not overlook the need to make lasting spiritual investments in others' lives. He said they had many guardians or teachers in the church, but not many spiritual fathers and mothers who were willing to spend time nurturing new believers: *"I am not writing this to shame you, but to warn you, as my dear children. Even though you have ten thousand guardians in Christ, you do not have many fathers...."* (1 Cor. 4:14-15). These Christians were immature as believers because they lacked true fathers to give them an identity, proper training, and nurturing. They needed spiritual fathers and mothers who were willing to spend time with them.

Many times, new believers never really grow to their full potential in God because they never had a spiritual parent to care for them. True spiritual parents are sincerely concerned about the welfare of their spiritual children.

THE HEARTS OF THE FATHERS

Why are spiritual parents who are willing to nurture spiritual children and help them achieve maturity so important? For one thing, it is a fulfillment of the Lord's promise in the last days to *"...turn the hearts of the fathers to their children, and the hearts of the children to their fathers..."* (Mal. 4:6).

The Lord wants to restore harmony among fathers and their children, both naturally and spiritually, so that fathers can freely impart their inheritance to the next generation. He wants spiritual fathers and mothers to take up the mantle to train their children so that they no longer flounder in the sea of life. Children need to have parents in their lives who will provide the character they need and tell them that they are valuable—gifts from God. Parents need to put expectation into their children's hearts so that they will believe in themselves.

Paul says in First Corinthians 4:17 that he is going to send Timothy to the Corinthian church because he would *"remind you [the Corinthians] of my way of life in Christ Jesus."* As a spiritual father, Paul faithfully trained Timothy. Now Timothy was ready to impart *his* spiritual fatherhood to the Corinthian church. Christian believers need to see spiritual fathering and mothering modeled so that they can be equipped to pass on a legacy to the next generation of believers.

Paul trained Timothy, his beloved and trustworthy spiritual son, and now Timothy was coming to train them. Paul trusted Timothy to help the Corinthian church because Paul had trained him like a son. With this example, they would soon be producing their own spiritual sons and daughters. This kind of mentoring relationship was a spiritual investment that would continue to multiply as equipped and mature believers went out into the world to spread the Gospel.

GROWTH STAGES

According to the Bible, we go through life in stages—as little children, young men, and fathers. At each point in our journey, we function in a particular way and have distinct tasks to perform. John addresses all three spiritual stages in First John 2:12-14:

> *I write to you, little children, because your sins are forgiven you for His name's sake. I write to you, fathers, because you have known Him who is from the beginning. I write to you, young men, because you have overcome the wicked one. I*

write to you, little children, because you have known the Father. I have written to you, fathers, because you have known Him who is from the beginning. I have written to you, young men, because you are strong, and the word of God abides in you, and you have overcome the wicked one (NKJV).

Fatherhood is the cry of God's heart. Since fatherhood is so crucial to God's divine order, He established a natural training ground consisting of "growth stages." Baby Christians grow to fatherhood as they progress through each of these stages. Only then can they receive the heart and revelation of a father or mother.

Our stages as babies in Christ, as young men and women, and as spiritual fathers and mothers have nothing to do with our chronological age but everything to do with how we eventually progress on to spiritual maturity. Children are expected to grow up. Only then can they become fathers and mothers.

If we fail to take the next steps to become spiritual parents, we remain spiritual babies—spiritually immature and lacking parenting skills. It is sad, but it is this scenario which is often the case in the Church. Many times there is no provision for believers to develop within our church systems.

Nevertheless, with the restoration of New Testament Christianity, as people meet together in small groups, God is providing an ideal setting to develop spiritual parents. Each person is given the opportunity to "do the work of ministry" and to connect in vital relationships with each other. Through modeling and impartation, spiritual reproduction happens naturally.

God's intention is to bring new believers to the place of spiritual fatherhood and motherhood after going through spiritual childhood and young adulthood. Paul the apostle made it his concern to instruct everyone properly so they could be grounded in the faith, *"...teaching every man in all wisdom, that we may present every man perfect in Christ Jesus"* (Col. 1:28 NKJV).

The Lord's call has not changed. Every believer, after being equipped, can become a spiritual parent. Meanwhile, we have to progress through stages of growth.

FROM CHILDHOOD TO YOUNG ADULTHOOD

Spiritual babies in the Body of Christ are wonderful! According to First John 2:12, they are children whose sins are forgiven. This forgiveness of sin puts them in fellowship with God and other believers. Spiritual children or new believers are alive to what they can receive from their Savior. They freely ask the Father when they have a need. Did you ever notice that new believers can pray prayers that seem to be theologically unsound, yet God answers almost every prayer that a new believer prays? The Father is quick to take care of these little ones.

A new believer's focus is forgiveness of sins, getting to Heaven, and getting to know the Father. Like natural babies, they know their Father, although it is not necessarily a thorough knowledge of God. A new believer will often act like a natural child with the marks of immaturity, including instability and gullibility. They will need constant assurance and care. They often do the unexpected because they are still learning what it means to follow Jesus. Spiritual parents are happy to spend extra time with spiritual children in order to guide them in the right direction.

But what happens when spiritual babies do not grow up? Not only new believers are spiritual babies in the Church today. Older Christians who lack spiritual maturity are "adults in age" but "babies in spiritual growth." They may be 20, 30, 40, or 50 years of age: Christian believers for years who have never spiritually matured. They live self-centered lifestyles, complaining, fussing, and throwing temper-tantrums when things do not go their way. Some do not accept the fact that God loves them for who they are. Others may wallow in self-pity when they fail. Many spiritual children in our churches today desperately need to grow up and move on to the next stage as spiritual young men and women.

Spiritual young men and women no longer have to be spoon-fed. According to First John 2:14, the Word of God abides in them, and they have learned to feed on the Word to overcome the wicked one. They don't need to run to others in the church to care for them like babies because they have learned how to apply the Word to their own lives. When the devil tempts them, they know what to do to overcome him. They use God's Word effectively and powerfully.

Spiritual young men and women must be encouraged (see 1 Tim. 4:12). They are strong in the Word and Spirit. They have learned to use the strength of spiritual discipline, prayer, and the study of the Word. They are alive to what they can do for Jesus.

On the other hand, the temptations of spiritual youth may be a trap for those who have not yet developed a strong sense of right and wrong. Youth are cautioned to run from their youthful passions that might lead to scandal (see 2 Tim. 2:22).

Spiritual young men or women may have attained a certain level of spiritual maturity, but they are not yet spiritual parents. They sometimes can become arrogant and dogmatic. After returning from the latest seminar or after reading a recent book, they may think that they have all of the answers. They need to be tempered by parenthood. They must become fathers and mothers to experience its joys and disciplines. Again, it bears repeating: becoming a spiritual parent has nothing to do with chronological age; it is a spiritual age.

SPIRITUAL FATHERS AND MOTHERS DEFINED

Just how do spiritual young men and women grow up to become spiritual fathers and mothers? There is only one way—to have children. You can become a spiritual parent either by natural birth (fathering someone you have personally led to Christ) or by adoption (fathering someone who is already a believer but needs to be mentored). Paul led Onesimus to Christ personally, so Onesimus was his natural spiritual son (see Philem. 1:10). Timothy was also Paul's spiritual son, but by spiritual "adoption" because Timothy came to Christ earlier through the influence of his mother and grandmother (see Acts 16).

Spiritual fathers and mothers are mature believers who have grown and matured in their Christian walk; they are called *fathers* according to First John 2:13: *"I write to you, fathers, because you have known Him who is from the beginning...."* This implies a profound and thorough knowledge of Jesus through knowing His Word. It also implies a deep sense of acquaintance with Him, by having a passion for Jesus.

Mature Christians are awake to their calling to be like Jesus—to be a father like God's Son. They understand what it takes to be a spiritual parent and are willing to become one.

One of the greatest catalysts to maturity as a Christian is to become a spiritual parent. Even if prospective spiritual parents do

301

not feel ready to become parents, as they take a step of faith and draw on the help and advice of their own spiritual mom and dad, they will find great success and fulfillment.

Spiritual fathers and mothers could be called *mentors* or *coaches* because they are in a place to help sons and daughters negotiate the obstacles of their spiritual journeys. A coach is someone who wants to see you win. A coach tells you that you can make it.

Simply stated, my favorite definition of a spiritual father or mother is the following: a spiritual father or mother helps a spiritual son or daughter to reach his or her God-given potential.

With mature spiritual parents at their side, sons and daughters' will grow strong and learn quickly and naturally by example. The parent teaches, trains, sets a good example, and provides a role model. Spiritual parents raise their children's awareness of attitudes or behaviors in their lives that need to be changed. They help new believers take an honest look at their lives and make adjustments so that their actions and behaviors can change.

OUR INHERITANCE OF SPIRITUAL CHILDREN

Regardless of our own experience—whether or not we have had a spiritual father or mother—we can become a spiritual father or mother to someone the Lord has placed in our lives. Every believer can make a decision to co-labor with Jesus and make disciples by becoming a spiritual father or mother to someone who needs our assistance to grow in the Lord.

So how do we begin? The early Christians did not haphazardly "share their faith." Instead, people were built together, each doing a job, working as a team to accomplish the Great Commission. God will place people in our lives that He wants us to reach out to. As we commit ourselves to train them, they will become conformed to Jesus' likeness. As new believers grow in Christ, they also will begin to make disciples, following the parent's example. Abraham was 99 years old when God gave him the promise that he would be the *"father of many nations"* (Gen. 17:4). Galatians 3:29 says that those who belong to Christ are *"Abraham's seed, and heirs according to the promise."* Therefore, as believers, God wants to birth in us "nations," too. These "nations" or groups of people, who come to know God because of our influence, will be our spiritual lineage—they are our posterity in God's Kingdom. We have been promised it because we are children of promise. Our God desires to give us a spiritual posterity.

Years ago, I was a spiritual father to Bill, now a missionary in the Caribbean. When I visited him in Barbados, Bill told me an interesting history of that island nation. Many of the people who now live in Barbados originally came as slaves from West Africa, specifically from the nation of the Gambia. Today, native Barbadians are being sent out from Barbados as missionaries to the Gambia. Then he said something that moved me deeply, "Larry, do you realize that the people being reached in the Gambia are part of your spiritual heritage? You were one of my spiritual fathers." At the time when I was a spiritual father to Bill, I was a young man myself, a chicken farmer who led a Bible study of young people. Bill had gone into the world and trained others to go, and the results mushroomed! I was deeply moved! It was as if I was the recipient of a large inheritance!

LEAVE A LEGACY

The promise of spiritual children is for every Christian. God has placed us here on earth because He has called us to become spiritual fathers and mothers in our generation. With this comes the expectation that our spiritual children will have more spiritual children and continue into infinity.

Our inheritance will be all of the spiritual children that we can some day present to Jesus Christ: *"For what is our hope, our joy, or the crown in which we will glory in the presence of our Lord Jesus when He comes? Is it not you? Indeed, you are our glory and joy"* (1 Thess. 2:19-20). No matter what you do—whether you are a housewife, a student, a worker in a factory, a pastor of a church, or the head a large corporation—you have the divine blessing and responsibility to birth spiritual children, grandchildren, and great grandchildren. You are called to impart to others the rich inheritance that God has promised.

If we would get serious about making disciples one at a time and training them so that they could go and make more disciples, it would not take long for every person on the face of the earth to be confronted with the truth of Jesus Christ. This scriptural principle is so simple, yet many times God's people have failed to obey this Great Commission from our Lord Jesus. God has called us and given us His priority to make disciples.

God uses the principle of multiplication through spiritual fathering and mothering. When you and I are obedient to Him, reaching out to one, two, three, four, or more people whom the Lord places in our lives, we will literally see God's Kingdom being established over the whole world. God wants to establish His Kingdom in our generation through the principle of multiplication through spiritual parenting. God's Kingdom is built as we love people and spend time with them.

Now that you have learned the basic foundations of the Christian life through this *Biblical Foundation Series*, pray about helping someone else grow in the Lord and teaching them what you have learned.[2]

I believe an end-time sweeping revival is just around the corner. God's people need to be alert and ready to accommodate the great harvest that this will bring into the Kingdom of God. Spiritual parents must be ready to obey His call and to take young Christians under their wings.

We are containers of the Holy Spirit, and God is going to pour His Spirit out on us that flows to others. Acts 2:17 tells us, *"'In the last days,' God says, 'I will pour out My Spirit on all people. Your sons and daughters will prophesy, your young men will see visions, your old men will dream dreams.'"*

Someday, you and I will stand before the Living God. When I stand before the Lord, I do not want to stand there by myself. How about you? Let's stand there with a multitude of our spiritual children, grandchildren, and their future descendants. The Lord wants to give you a spiritual legacy. God has called you to be a spiritual parent who mentors and trains others to do the same!

ENDNOTES

1. For more on spiritual fathers and mothers, read Larry Kreider *Authentic Spiritual Mentoring* (Ventura, CA: Regal Books, 2008); www.h2hp.com.

2. If you desire more training to become a spiritual father or mother, I recommend my video training entitled *The Cry for Spiritual Fathers and Mothers*, www.h2hp.com.

BEING A SPIRITUAL FATHER OR MOTHER
REFLECTION QUESTIONS

1. Do you sense a need for a spiritual father or mother to equip you to "go into the world"? Are you willing to become a spiritual father or mother?

2. What are the growth stages for a new Christian to become a spiritual parent? What happens if we fail to go through these stages?

3. What are some characteristics of spiritual children? Of spiritual young men and women?

4. What is our spiritual legacy? How does having and becoming a spiritual parent help you obey the Great Commission?

ADDITIONAL RESOURCES

WWW.DCFI.ORG

BUILDING YOUR PERSONAL HOUSE OF PRAYER

If you love to pray, or you need to pray more effectively, this book will change your prayer life forever. Your entire approach to prayer is about to improve! By Larry Kreider, 254 pages: $15.99 ISBN: 978-0-7684-2662-5

HEARING GOD 30 DIFFERENT WAYS

The Lord speaks to us in ways we often miss, including through the Bible, prayer, circumstances, spiritual gifts, conviction, His character, His peace, and even in times of silence. Take 30 days and discover how God's voice can become familiar to you as you develop a loving relationship with Him. By Larry Kreider, 224 pages: $14.99 ISBN: 978-1-886973-76-3

AUTHENTIC SPIRITUAL MENTORING

There is a desperate need for spiritually mature men and women to mentor younger believers to be fully equipped and faithful servants of Christ. Whether you are looking for a spiritual mentor or desiring to become one, this book is for you! By Larry Kreider, 224 pages: ISBN: 978-0-8307-4413-8

Speak Lord! I'm Listening

Jesus said, "My sheep hear my voice," but many Christians do not know how to hear from God. In this practical, story-rich guidebook, international teacher Larry Kreider shows believers how to develop a listening relationship with the Lord. It explores the multiple ways Christians can hear the voice of God in today's world, offering real-life examples—not theory—of how God teaches His followers to listen, with tips in each chapter for distinguishing His voice from the noise of satan's interference. Christians across the denominational spectrum will develop a closer and deeper relationship with God as they learn 50 unique ways to listen to Him. You will realize that God was speaking to you all along but, like the disciples on the road to Emmaus, you didn't know it was Him! By Larry Kreider, 224 pages: ISBN: 978-0-830746-12-5

Exercise the Fruit of the Spirit and Get Fit for Life

This book encourages you to take a spiritual health check of your life to see if you are producing the Bible's nine exercises for spiritual wellness as mentioned in Galatians 5:22-23 and expressed in the believer as growing the fruit of the Spirit. By Larry Kreider and Sam Smucker, ISBN: 978-1-886973-93-0

The Biblical Role of Elders for Today's Church

New Testament principles for equipping church leadership teams: Why leadership is needed, what their qualifications and responsibilities are, how they should be chosen, how elders function as spiritual fathers and mothers, how they are to make decisions, resolve conflicts, and more. By Larry Kreider, Ron Myer, Steve Prokopchak, and Brian Sauder, 274 pages: ISBN: 978-1-886973-62-6

HELPING YOU BUILD CELL CHURCHES MANUAL

A complete biblical blueprint for small groups, this manual covers 51 topics! Includes study and discussion questions. Use for training small group leaders or personal study. Compiled by Brian Sauder and Larry Kreider, 224 pages: ISBN: 978-1-886973-38-1

CHURCH PLANTING AND LEADERSHIP TRAINING

(LIVE OR VIDEO SCHOOL WITH LARRY KREIDER AND OTHERS)

Prepare now for a lifetime of ministry and service to others. The purpose of this school is to train the leaders our world is desperately looking for. We provide practical information as well as Holy Spirit empowered impartation and activation. Be transformed and prepared for a lifetime of ministry and service to others.

If you know where you are called to serve...church, small group, business, public service, marketplace, or if you simply want to grow in your leadership ability—our goal is to help you build a biblical foundation to be led by the Holy Spirit and pursue your God-given dreams. **For a complete list of classes and venues, visit www.dcfi.org.**

SCHOOL OF GLOBAL TRANSFORMATION

(SEVEN-MONTH RESIDENTIAL DISCIPLESHIP SCHOOL)

Be equipped for a lifetime of service in the church, marketplace and beyond! The School of Global Transformation is a seven-month residential discipleship school that runs September through March. Take seven months to satisfy your hunger for more of God.

Experience His love in a deeper way than you ever dreamed possible. He has a distinctive plan and purpose for your life. We are committed to helping students discover destiny in Him and prepare them to transform the world around them.

For details visit www.dcfi.org.

SEMINARS

One-day Seminars with Larry Kreider and other DOVE Christian Fellowship International authors and leaders:

Building a Biblical Foundation for Your Life

Building Your Personal House of Prayer

How to Fulfill Your Calling as a Spiritual Father/Mother

How to Build Healthy Leadership Teams

How to Hear God—30 Different Ways

Called Together Couple Mentoring

How to Build Small Groups—Basics

How to Grow Small Groups—Advanced

Counseling Basics

Effective Fivefold Ministry Made Practical

Starting House Churches

Planting Churches Made Practical

How to Live in Kingdom Prosperity

How to Equip and Release Prophetic Ministry

For more information about DCFI seminars,
call 800-848-5892.

E-mail: seminars@dcfi.org

CONTACT INFORMATION FOR
SPEAKING ENGAGEMENTS:

Larry Kreider, International Director
DOVE Christian Fellowship International
11 Toll Gate Road
Lititz, PA 17543
Website: www.dcfi.org
E-mail: LarryK@dcfi.org

Additional copies of this book and other
book titles from DESTINY IMAGE are
available at your local bookstore.

Call toll-free: 1-800-722-6774.

Send a request for a catalog to:

Destiny Image® Publishers, Inc.
P.O. Box 310
Shippensburg, PA 17257-0310

Speaking to the Purposes of God for This
Generation and for the Generations to Come.

For a complete list of our titles,
visit us at www.destinyimage.com.